# LIBRARY MEETS BOOK FAIR

## Other books by Glenn Martin

*Stories/Reflections on experience*

The Ten Thousand Things (2010)

Sustenance (2011)

To the Bush and Back to Business (2012)

The Big Story Falls Apart (2014)

The Quilt Approach: A Tasmanian Patchwork (2020)

Long Time Approaching (2023)

Travel with a Pen (2023)

*Books on ethics and values*

Human Values and Ethics in the Workplace (2010)

The Little Book of Ethics: A Human Values Approach (2011)

The Concise Book of Ethics (2012)

A Foundation for Living Ethically (2020)

Future: The Spiritual Story of Humanity (2020)

*Books on family history*

A Modest Quest (2017)

The Search for Edward Lewis (2018)

They Went to Australia (2019)

No Gold in Melbourne: A Scottish Family in Australia (2021)

All the Rivers Come Together: Tracing Family (2022)

*Poetry collections*

Flames in the Open (2007)

Love and Armour (2007)

Volume 4: I in the Stream (2017)

Volume 3: That Was Then: The Early Poems Project (2019)

The Way Is Open (2020)

*Local histories*

Places in the Bush: A History of Kyogle Shire (1988)

The Kyogle Public School Centenary Book (1995)

# LIBRARY
## MEETS BOOK FAIR

Glenn Martin

G.P. Martin Publishing

Published 2024 by G.P. Martin Publishing

Website: www.glennmartin.com.au

Contact: info@glennmartin.com.au

Book layout and cover design by the author

Typeset in Sitka 11 pt

Printed by Lulu.com

Cover images and design by the author.

ISBN: 978 0 6459543 1 9 (pbk.)

A catalogue record for this book is available from the National Library of Australia

# Contents

## First Words

The author has written over twenty books, on a variety of subjects. But he also has a personal library, which has accumulated over a period of more than fifty years. It has followed him from place to place, and now it has taken root. It has been regularly augmented from bookshops, second-hand bookshops, online purchases, and occasional fortuitous sales, such as at libraries. But the book fairs of Sydney have changed the conditions of acquisition. Formerly, to buy a lot of books was a rich person's folly. Now, it can be a poor person's bounty.

However, time is not as malleable as money, and one should not buy more books than one can conceivably read. Some perspicacity is still called for. This book is about the grounds of perspicacity.

# 1   Introduction: About My Library

I have my own library. Is it a home library, a private library or a personal library? There could be arguments about this. Regardless, I have a library. It occupies a building separate from the house. The other half of the building is a garage. Well, it is supposed to be a garage, but it is now a workshop. I built a carport for the car so that it would not sulk.

The library part used to be the workshop for a man who made stained-glass windows. The library and the house have several samples: the double doors of the library, and double windows in the bathroom. They are exquisite and delightful.

The library is not confined to the garage. It also occupies several parts of the house – the loungeroom, the hallway, the dining room and the ex-bedroom that I use for an office. My bedside cabinet has a stack of books on it, but I try to limit this. I claim to have some discipline. These books are only for current reading (defined as, probably sometime this year).

There is a loose distinction between the house-library and the garage-library (or, the "library proper"). Fiction goes in the house; non-fiction goes in the library proper. Once, I went to a book fair and they had a section labelled "Non-Fiction". I did not find many books at that book fair. There has to be a little more discrimination than that.

In contrast, at the last Knox Grammar book fair I went to, there were printed copies of all the different categories they had, scattered around. There were fifty-eight categories, and the list was ordered alphabetically, linked to tables marked with large letters. This is reputed to be the largest book fair in Sydney.

In my library proper, there are categories, although the categories are loose and I am currently wrestling with how to improve the organisation of my books. My purpose is pragmatic. I regard my library as a working library, and I need to be able to find the right books for whatever project is in my mind at the time.

I recently read the book *Library* by Matthew Battles (discussed below), and he has both inspired me and provoked me to return to this question, which has lurked for years. Many years ago I attempted a simplified Dewey system, but to be honest, other categories which are not strictly Dewey tend to intervene. I have a shelf of school mathematics books that reflect the years I spent as a mathematics teacher. I have a short shelf which contains books that are taller than usual, so that is an odd assortment. Moreover, these sections are not in sequential order under the Dewey system. The mathematics books are on a high shelf because I don't consult them often.

The list of categories from the Knox Grammar book fair was something of a relief, because it gave permission to categories that were simply popular. Most book fairs have sections on Royalty and Military, neither of which are of interest to me. The nice thing is that it simplifies my looking; I don't have to look at them.

There are basic questions regarding libraries. I think I found Matthew Battles' book because I was ready for it. He asks the question over thousands of years: why the library? What is its purpose? And of course, the answer was different at different times of history. But to be pragmatic rather than philosophical, why do I still have mathematics books? I have not taught mathematics for many years. Why don't I simply give the books away; for example, to a book fair?

To be harsh, you could argue that the books in my library are simply photographs of me at different times of my life. The library is like a photo album. Maybe. You could argue that. But I have counter-examples. One example involves a printed record rather than a book, but it serves my purpose.

When I first left school, I went to the University of New South Wales (UNSW) to study Civil Engineering. I thought that this was what I should do (note the word "should"). However, after two years, I realised that I didn't have to just make it for two more years. If I passed, which I would, I would then have to be an engineer for the next forty or so years. At that point I realised that I did not want to be an engineer.

This is relevant because, after numerous changes and many years, I became an expert in building educational websites. Then I went for a job at a college where I would be building websites for an engineering degree. I could demonstrate my expertise in building educational websites easily enough, but how could I convince them that I could handle engineering material?

I went to my filing cabinet and pulled out the transcript of my UNSW studies. Although I had not completed my degree, I had successfully completed the first two years, and years ago I had gone to the trouble of obtaining a neat transcript of those studies. I made about ten copies of it and took it to the interview. When the inevitable question arose: "How will you be able to manage the engineering content?" I simply handed around the copies of the transcript. I got the job.

This is an object lesson on the value of records – and books! On another occasion, I was writing something that begged a reference to the counter-culture of the early 1970s. I had the quote in my mind, from Theodore Roszak's wonderful book, *The Making of the Counter Culture* (1972). It had opened my mind to many new things. It had made it possible for me to make sense of society at the time from a fresh perspective.

I knew exactly where the book was on my shelves, so I could go straight to it. Then I knew that the quote I wanted was on the right-hand side of the page about halfway through the book. I found the quote within a few minutes. This is another object lesson about the value of a library, as long as you know what is in your library, and as long as you care about what is in the books. The books need to be adding to your understanding – of something in particular, or of life overall.

This story also evokes one of my reservations about reorganising my library. I had a physical memory of where Roszak's books was. If I move it to a more "sensible" location, chances are that I won't be able to find the book anymore. Logic on one day is not necessarily the same as logic on another day. How many times do we find ourselves unable to find an object because we have moved it to somewhere where we will be able to find it more easily?

## 2    Library Meets Book Fairs

Why are book fairs of interest to me? My interest is not the same as that of other people. Book dealers (for example, owners of second-hand book stores) turn up in droves on the morning of the first day of book fairs. They are focused and intent. I have learned to avoid the first few hours. My perusing is slow and thoughtful, and I do not like to be elbowed.

Obviously, I am not concerned about "missing out" on some rare or unique book. I am content to see what turns up. In any case, the book dealers are looking for something that will sell fast. I am looking for books that most people would overlook. Nor am I interested in first editions or books that are pristine, unmarked. One of my joys is to find books that have a previous owner's name inscribed in them, or even better, a book owner's name plate. Or, an inscription from a gift-giver Here's one:

"Mothers Day 2009. Dear Mum, we heard that you want to write a book so we boght this to help you. Love, Finn + Stella. Happy Mothers Day" (The book was *Writing down the Bones: Freeing the Writer Within* by Natalie Goldberg. I preserved the spelling.)

When I consider my reasons for going to book fairs and buying books, one of my thoughts is that I am not collecting books. Others (including my children) find this hard to believe. Isn't it obvious that I am collecting books? Hasn't the number of bookshelves grown over the years? Have I given any books away?

My response is that to answer those questions, we have to consider my reasons, not just the traffic. The traffic will tell you nothing. However, the question we are considering at the moment is why I go to book fairs. The answer is not anything as tasteless as "addiction".

I left Sydney when I was twenty-four, and I did not come back to Sydney until I was forty-seven. I wasn't eager to come back to Sydney, but it is okay, and there are some benefits. Firstly, there are concerts in Sydney – big-name groups and performers from overseas; and then there are book fairs.

Note, I did not come back to Sydney in order to be able to go to book fairs. They were a discovery after I arrived. It was one of those discoveries when you think, "Oh, my goodness!" and "What could that mean?" I already had a library, and it had been with me everywhere: from Sydney to Mackay, then Wyndham Creek in Kyogle, Horseshoe Creek in Kyogle, and now back in Sydney. It had grown somewhat, but it still had to be kept in check.

In my current home, finally, I had space where I could breathe a little, and after a while the ex-stained-glass workshop became what it was meant to be: a library. I built shelves, having learnt from my former strictures. All the shelves should be tall enough to accommodate most books, otherwise any attempt to categorise them is undone by the height of the shelves. I had had plenty of experience of that. In the end, the main principle of categorisation becomes the height of the book: small, medium, tall. My chosen shelf height for my 'permanent' library was 320 millimetres. I had examined the height of bookshelves in public and university libraries as well.

As I said, I have only one small shelf for taller-than-usual books. It is just 570 millimetres wide, and after all these years it is still adequate. However, the point of book fairs was not to make my library bigger. That would be crass. I came back to Sydney because I had got a job as a writer, writing about management topics for a publishing company. I had management experience and I had a Bachelor degree in business, but for this job I also needed to be articulate and well-read.

I wanted to be able to write from a broad understanding and a decent foundation of knowledge of current management literature. I spent lots of time at libraries and in bookshops, but once I discovered book fairs, I realised that I could acquire relevant books cheaply and keep them, rather than borrowing them from a library for three or four weeks. This meant I could mark them and tag them, and refer back to them. (I had learned my lesson from the Theodore Roszak book.)

I wasn't trying to be smart, and I wasn't trying to pretend that I had read everything. I simply wanted to reflect a sound understanding of the topics I was writing about. In my reading, I was trying to integrate the various writers' perspectives into a viable and helpful viewpoint. By this time I was developing my own perspective as an offering. You can tell when a writer is being superficial and doesn't understand the depths and contradictions that reality embodies. I wanted to offer more than that.

I believe I succeeded in this. People would tell me I was "a good writer", which I understood to mean I expressed the qualities I described in the previous paragraph.

Is it starting to make sense now? I went to book fairs because I was pursuing trains of thought, and I acquired books that would extend and enlarge those trains of thought. Some of the value was immediate, and some of it had a broader cast. For example, I decided that I wanted some basic textbooks on sociology. I had studied it in my second unfinished degree, a Bachelor of Arts at the University of Sydney. I thought there were useful concepts in sociology, and I should have some books that gave me the basic concepts and dynamics of the field.

Sometimes, I was pushed a bit further. Recently, I remembered the concept of "reference groups", because I think this idea is often helpful in understanding human behaviour. I have three sociology textbooks, but "reference groups" was only mentioned in two of them, and the explanation amounted to only one paragraph in each. And here was I thinking that the concept was a basic sociology construct. I ended up resorting to the internet where, of course, I did find useful and relevant content.

However, I was born in 1950; I am not a "digital native", although I can navigate the country well enough. I can't imagine having a Theodore Roszak moment in the digital world. I wonder if book fairs will even exist in twenty years' time. According to the prevailing mythology, everything is going digital. Perhaps my entire library is anachronistic. But my argument is: nevertheless! I am here. That is my argument. I will persist. My library is a living thing, and it is an extension of me. No apology.

For me, going to a book fair is a way of immersing myself in a field of consciousness. There is what I am thinking about at the moment, and there are all the things I have thought about beforehand, and what sense I am making of these things, both deliberately and beneath the surface of consciousness. This may make more sense if I say I am a writer of books. The swirls of thought are liable to be developed into books on particular subjects. Of course, all the thoughts have an under-swirl of feelings, as well as conceptions about what I think is right and wrong (and alternative synonyms for that).

What do I buy at book fairs? It depends! I only take one shopping bag in with me, so I am setting a limit from the outset. Why? Is it about putting a limit on greed? No, it is not that. It is about, notionally, at least, being able to digest what I buy. I am not a collector. My intent is to read what I buy, at some point. I have books that I have finally read after ten years, because they suddenly became relevant to what I was working on.

There are a few books I haven't read yet because I still find them a bit intimidating. Sometimes I will pick up such a book and leaf through it with the idea of seeing how it fits with what I understand now. Maybe I will appreciate it more this time, and allocate it to my reading pile. When you accept the hidden connections between things, the weird flow of knowledge in the intangible universe at all times, you just have to relax. You can't possible control all this.

Here is a measure of the impossibility of controlling everything, and the impossibility of resisting. I was walking past a bookshop. What admirable constraint, you think. But this bookshop has shelves outside the bookshop, mostly for second-hand and old books, so it wouldn't matter so much if someone stole one. A book on one of these shelves caught my eye. It's tough to resist, isn't it?

I bought the book. It was about a famous Chinese author in the 1930s, Lin Yutang. From Shanghai, he went to Harvard University in his twenties to study for a PhD. He said that he went into the Widener Library at Harvard and felt that he had come alive for the first time. I could really appreciate that sentiment.

But the point of the story is this. After reading that, I was at another book fair, the one where I bought the book, *Library* – the one by Matthew Battles. I opened it up, and on the first couple of pages it mentioned the Widener Library. So I bought the book. Bear in mind that I had never heard of the Widener Library before this episode. I know some readers hate stories like this. They immediately fling the word 'coincidence' at you, scornfully.

My response is: "Forget about coincidence. You are wasting your life. Start listening and watching the patterns that are occurring."

Earlier this year I went to a book fair and got the idea of noting the books I found that I already owned. I had noticed this before, but had just taken it as a cue to ignore the book and move on. This time, I decided to take note. It was at Galston (northwest of Sydney) book fair, and I found three books. All were of note in any case, because they were unusual books.

This is where the idea happened, so I was curious as to what would happen if I had the idea from the start of a book fair, and used my mobile phone to take photos of the covers. The next book fair was at Brookvale, on the northern beaches, and I discovered fourteen books. Did this mean that I had enough books at home, and I should stop going to book fairs? Did the subjects of the books mean anything? Were the topics things that were on my mind at the moment?

You could also ask, how did I know I already owned these books? You assume I have a lot of books. Well, I probably have about five thousand, but it's not unlimited. Only on one or two occasions have I bought a book that I already owned. But do I have books where I am not aware that I have multiple copies? I don't think so.

There have only been a couple of occasions where I have not been able to find a book that I know I own. Sometimes this might be because I have lent a book out, but I am not a lending library. If I lend a book, either it comes back eventually or it is lost (happily) in the flow of knowledge and learning between people. But yes, I do like to get books back (this is my reminder to friends). There is the integrity of the collection to consider.

The next book fair I went to was the Knox Grammar one, and I found nineteen books that I already owned. Was this because it was the biggest book fair in Sydney? Was it because I took my time and perused all the tables at leisure? Or was it because I was now tuned in to my new quest? Perhaps all of the above. Again, do the topics indicate something of relevance to my current thinking? Or is there something in the fact that all these books have come onto the book market now?

Mostly, I think books turn up at book fairs because their most recent owners are lightening the load. Downsizing has become a trend these days. There is considerable economics as well as ideology behind it. I accept that as people get older, and their children have left home, they start to feel their homes as empty, and yearn for something smaller. But also, there is the thought of capitalising on the larger house and space they have, moving into something smaller and living on the cash surplus.

There are also the books that are the result of a death. A husband or a wife has died, and it is the trigger for getting rid of the book collection. So, a book that has lain dormant on the shelves for thirty or forty years comes back into circulation. I am not interested in collecting their cast-offs. My interest is a dynamic one: is it relevant to what I am thinking about at the moment? Does it extend my boundaries?

Perhaps, too, there is something in the lifecycle of the books themselves that favours their turning up at certain times. For example, a book that is a thriller might turn up just a year or two after its release. That is because people buy it to read on the train, and once they've read it, they are finished with it. It's not a book to keep, so they give it away. and it turns up at a book fair.

But, in looking for books that I already own, I am reversing my parameters. This quest evokes my entire reading past, and it raises the question, are these books relevant at the moment? Or at least, what is their place in my history? Sometimes, there is a story about the book rather than about its content. For example, at the Knox Grammar book fair, I found *Sinning across Spain*, by Ailsa Piper. I didn't really like the title, because I think it misrepresented the content, and I thought it was a marketer's lame attempt at alliteration. However, I enjoyed the book; I thought the story had substance and meaning; it had heart as well as good humour.

The reason this book stands out in my memory was that I went to a book festival at St Albans, northwest of Sydney (or was it a writers' festival, or a readers' festival?) and Ailsa spoke there. She talked about the story behind the book, and she was engaging. She had followed the pilgrims' trail across Spain from Granada to the seaside cliffs at Finisterre. With her she "carried the sins" of her friends, as the Christian pilgrims traditionally did. From memory, I had not heard of the book before the festival, but I bought it at the festival. The festival also remains in my mind because the following year, the organisers decided they had had enough, and the festival did not happen again (and then COVID happened, so they were prescient).

Do I have an answer to my question? What I found interesting about the books that turned up was that they came from such a variety of time frames. Some of them were of very recent interest. Karen Armstrong wrote *Fields of Blood*, which is subtitled "Religion and the history of violence". It was published in 2014. I looked at it when I was writing my book, *Future* (published 2020). I thought, without much depth, that it was an insider's attempt to whitewash Christianity. We all know about the Inquisition, the Crusades, and the treatment of witches.

However, I have since read Herbert Benson's book, *Timeless Healing*, and he mentioned her in a favourable way, indicating that she had worthwhile insights into belief, institutions and politics. I have decided to approach her again in a more substantive, unbiassed way. Yes, life is full of shortcuts: dismissing books because there are so many of them!

On the other hand, I found books that took me back to my early twenties. I had purchased *Modern Art and the Death of a Culture* by H.R. Rookmaaker when I was still at the University of Sydney and was wrestling with big ideas. I didn't delve into it very much. I found a certain emptiness about schools of thought: abstract surrealism, cubism, expressionism, nihilism. The author was a Christian, and I bought the book at the Scripture Book Centre in Sydney. The picture on the cover is by Francis Bacon, called "Head VI" and it is horrible to look at – a screaming man with the top of his head blown off.

I turned from this whole struggle of ideologies towards a back-to-earth lifestyle. Now, I am wondering why the book is raising its head again. Is it time to give fresh consideration to that world of turmoil? The other books I have found have certainly had points of resonance with my past. I am interested to follow their thread and see what shapes up.

# 3    A Scoring System for Attending Book Fairs

It was at the Galston book fair that I first had the idea of taking note of the books I knew I already owned. Perhaps noticing such books emphasised to me that I did have a substantial personal library. So, at the Galston book fair (Friday 23 June 2023), I realised that I could score this, and I scored "3". How so? I scored one for each book.

These were the books:

- *Green Mountains*, Bernard O'Reilly
- *The Story of Mankind*, Hendrik Willem Van Loon
- *The Importance of Living*, Lin Yutang.

I think that my scoring system, so far, is rather poor, but it's a start. It's deficient because I think each of my points is "pretty good", but I don't want to make the scoring system too complicated either. So, I will tell the stories about each book.

## 1.  Green Mountains

By Bernard O'Reilly

You could say that *Green Mountains* is an obscure historical story about a remote place in the mountains on the border between New South Wales and Queensland. Or you could say it is all the more interesting for that. The author, Bernard O'Reilly, was from a pioneering family living in the Lamington Ranges. In their secluded location, Bernard had established a guesthouse: O'Reilly's Hostel. The centrepiece of the book is the story of Bernard's actions that were instrumental in saving the lives of two people after a plane crash in the vicinity in 1937.

Plane journeys were becoming more regular in the late 1930s, but they were still only for the adventurous. The plane was a Stinson, built in America, purchased the year before by Airlines of Australia. It was considered to be modern and luxurious, with a cruising speed of 265 km/hr. The plane took off from Brisbane at 1:00 pm on Friday 19 February carrying two pilots and five passengers. It was expected in Sydney by 4:30 pm.

The weather was murky and unsettled, with patches of heavy rain and high winds. It did not arrive in Sydney before night-fall, and was reported as missing. The news was broadcast over the wireless. It was generally thought that the plane had crashed somewhere near Newcastle, so the search parties that eventuated were concentrated in that area.

Bernard O'Reilly heard the news broadcast at the guesthouse over the wireless and had a hunch that the plane had not made it over the mountains. He set out on horseback to search for the wreck. He found it on the second day in steep, dense scrub. Of the seven people who had been on board, five had died. There were two survivors, John Proud and Joseph Binstead. He rode to a nearby farm to summon help, and a rescue party was sent, on foot, to retrieve the survivors. The two pilots and two of the passengers had died instantly in the crash. A third passenger, Jim Westray, had been injured in the crash but he had set out to get help; he died after falling over a cliff.

The book also talks about Bernard's efforts to establish the guesthouse in Lamington Park. O'Reilly's still exists (2023) and is still secluded, beautiful and popular.

This book is of special interest to me because in 1988 I wrote a history of the Kyogle Shire for the Kyogle Shire Council: *Places in the Bush*. It was the first history of the shire that had been written since 1953, and that had been more of a "coffee table" book. The Kyogle Shire runs up to the New South Wales border with Queensland. While I was writing the book, several people said to me that the book would not be complete unless I included the story of the Stinson plane crash of 1937, and Bernard O'Reilly's part in the rescue of the survivors. The plane crash site was close to the border, so much so that the farm that Bernard rode to after he had found the survivors was in Collins Creek, Kyogle.

One of the people who had exhorted me to write the story offered to accompany me on a day trip to O'Reilly's Guesthouse and introduce me to the family. So, we drove up there one Saturday. It was a very beautiful place, nestled in the bush and high in the mountains. I heard the family's memories about their father's inspired hunch and the bush knowledge that guided his trek through the rugged mountains to find the crashed plane. I took my four-year-old son with me, although he doesn't have any memories of the occasion now.

The book: I had been told that Bernard had written the story of the plane crash and the rescue, but when I wrote the Kyogle history book, I did not have a copy of it. I picked up my information from browsing through copies of the local newspaper, the *Kyogle Examiner*.

This was before the days of digital information. The old copies of the newspaper were bound into large binders and kept in the back room of the *Examiner* office in Kyogle. I used to have to stand there at a big table and work my way through the papers page by page, taking notes in a notepad by hand.

When did I get Bernard O'Reilly's book?

I finally found a copy of the book after I moved to Sydney in late 1997, and subsequently discovered book fairs. At some point I found a paperback copy of *Green Mountains*. It's hard to say what year this edition was published; it is not stated. It was published by Envirobook, Sydney. It has a website, but the website does not give the year of this book's publication either. However, it can be said that it was published after Bernard's death in 1975.

I got even luckier at a later book fair. I came across the original hardback version of the book, which was printed in 1940 by W.R. Smith & Paterson, Brisbane (was it self-published?). Its original purchase price was nine shillings and sixpence. In the introduction, Bernard says that he had received many requests to tell the story. He says it was "a saga of courage and endurance on the part of both rescued and rescuers; furnishing another page in the growing history of Australian character and achievement."

So, for this book fair, Score = 1.

Having already obtained two prize-worthy copies of the book, I did not feel the need to buy the paperback at the most recent book fair.

## 2. The Story of Mankind
By Hendrik Willem Van Loon

The story about this book is also very worthy. I already had a copy of it, but in this case I did buy the new copy that I found. The main reason was that there was a huge time difference between the two editions. The one that I owned was published in 1999, while the one at the book fair was published fifty-eight years earlier, in 1941. Of course, I didn't know this when I was at the book fair, but I knew I had found a much earlier copy than the one I had.

My existing copy was a hardback with an impressive dust jacket. Interestingly, it bore a gold sticker which said it was the winner of the John Newbery Medal. Later, I looked this up. It was indeed auspicious. Van Loon was the first winner of the medal, which was established in 1921 by the Association for Library Services for Children. It was for "The Most Distinguished Contribution to American Literature for Children".

The much older copy that I found was also a hardback, also impressively done, with a striking border, and illustrations on both the front cover and the spine. Curiously, it did not say it had been the winner of the Newbery Medal. I suppose the book had already been printed.

Over the last few years, I have developed an interest in books that tell "the story of mankind" or, in more gender-neutral language, "the story of humanity". I don't ever hope to know everything about the history of humans on this planet, but I am interested in the point of view of the storytellers. This was one of the themes of my book *Future: The Spiritual Story of Humanity*, published in 2020. It piqued my interest that many of these writers saw humans as becoming bigger, stronger, smarter – an unstoppable tide, almost gods on earth.

Much as I can see and appreciate what we have learned to do, and how our lives, collectively, have materially improved, we have to reconcile this with the harm we have caused the planet, the continuing suffering of many people, and our seeming inability to correct our lust for consumption.

In the book *Future*, I wrestled with this conundrum. I don't think I resolved it, but I do think I threw the question into the spotlight for more rigorous consideration. I think the answer will require us to juggle contrary truths more ably. I think it will require us to take our foot off the accelerator: not everything is fixed by pushing forward ever more aggressively. And much is gained by learning contentment and compassion for others. Can we do this collectively?

What does Hendrik Willem Van Loon have to say? He was a Dutchman, and his book was first published in England in 1922. He tells the story, in the original edition, in sixty-three chapters, starting with the birth of the planet as a ball of flaming matter, succeeded by rain and the oceans. "Then one day the great wonder happened. What had been dead gave birth to life. The first living cell floated upon the waters of the sea."

Hendrik writes to engage the interest of children. He takes readers through the history of humanity as it was understood at the end of the First World War. He paints with a broad brush. For example, Chapter 50 is titled "How the newly founded national or dynastic states of Europe tried to make themselves rich" (in the seventeenth century). As I wrote in *Future*, in a book of this nature, it is hard to refrain from conveying the notion of history as a fascinating tale of adventure.

However, there seems to be some sense in trying to tell a broad-brush story, because it comes down to power, technologies and human motivations. Van Loon, in his final chapter written in 1921, points to the radical changes in the world wrought in the last (say) four hundred years that have thrust business and technology to the fore. The attitudes of people towards the changes this has made to their roles, that is, the nature of their work and their economic predicament, contend with the political structures that govern nations.

I was interested, of course, to compare what Van Loon had to say in 1921 about how we should view the world, and what his successors had to say in 1999. One element is the same: the Foreword. Van Loon described being taken up to the top of the tower of the Church of St. Lawrence in Rotterdam (in The Netherlands) at the age of twelve. He saw the whole city and the surrounding countryside below him. His comment is this: "Best of all, the wide view of the glorious past, which surrounded us on all sides, gave us new courage to face the problems of the future."

In the intervening years, I now learned, the book had been updated three times by professors of history from Yale University and New

York University. In the 1999 edition there were seventy-five chapters, taking us up to the end of the twentieth century. The book concludes that the conditions of life for most people on the planet have improved dramatically over the past hundred years. "We have every reason to hope and be optimistic that the first century of the new millennium will bring, not only further progress in science and technology, but a better life for an even greater percentage of the world's population" (p. 656).

In my book, *Future*, I wonder whether this will be enough. The final chapters of Van Loon's book (as added by the history professors) wonder whether it will become more critical than ever to "tame the savageness of man and make gentle the life of the world". The quote is taken from an impromptu speech in 1968 by Robert Kennedy upon the assassination of Martin Luther King. (The quotation is presumed to come from an ancient Greek classic written by Aeschylus, but as with many important things, the source has not been able to be verified.)

For my book-fair purposes, my interest was in going back in time to see what Van Loon had to say in 1921. I already knew what the later writers had to say in 1999.

For those interested in such things, the book was originally sold for ten shillings and sixpence, and it was given to Sally, "with love from Auntie Miriam". This was likely to have occurred during World War Two, as the book was published in December 1941, by Pitman Press in Bath, England. It was the thirteenth reprinting since 1922.

Score so far for this book fair = 2. And there is another book to review: *The Importance of Living* by Lin Yutang - another old book, first published in 1939.

### 3. The Importance of Living
By Lin Yutang

Although I already owned this book, I bought it again, and you might think my reasons were petty. The copy I have is perfectly satisfactory, and I was also pretty sure it was the same edition: in hardback, and not the first edition. The first Australian edition was in 1946, and I thought that the copy I had was a few years later, say 1952. The copy at the book fair was 1952. And I was right; when I got home, the two copies were both from 1952, registered at the G.P.O. in Adelaide for transmission by post as a book, printed in Adelaide by the Advertiser Printing Office.

What was my petty reason for buying the book again? The previous owner (I presume) had vandalised the book. On the title page, the author's name had had lettering carefully added so that it said "B. LINDYUTANGLE" and on the reverse title page it said "WORKS BY LINDYUTANGLEDUP". Perhaps the owner had been given the book for Christmas and was feeling mischievous about their possession. Perhaps they had wanted something else for Christmas, so they were feeling a bit peeved. Or maybe a younger sister or brother had surreptitiously taken the book and put their scallywag mark on it. A great deal of that family's history is evident here.

The new book was unvandalised. The only addition was the former owner's name "Sylvia Roach" on the title page, a perfectly acceptable addition, written in an adult's graceful running writing.

I must have been interested enough in the book to be bothered buying another copy of it. I was. It was curious to me that a Chinese man had written a philosophical-type book in America for American (and Australian) consumption. The Preface is signed by him in New York City on July 30, 1937. Isn't that intriguing? Of course, after five minutes of perusing, I could have decided that the book was boring and irrelevant.

However, he caught my interest with remarks I could relate to. He said he would have liked to write the entire book in the form of a dialogue like Plato's, but he did not do so because he thought that people might not read it, "and a writer after all wants to be read". By dialogue he meant long leisurely passages, not the short, sharp type of question and answer you find in a newspaper interview. When I bought the first copy of the book, I had had the reverse thought. I had recently written a book on ethics: *A Foundation for Living Ethically* (2020), and I thought it would be more digestible for readers if I wrote it as a dialogue between two people. I still think that.

Lin Yutang was modest about the foundation of his philosophy, and I liked that too. He said he had "travelled the bypaths" in his reading, often finding gems among obscure writers. "Technically speaking, my method and my training are all wrong, because I do not read philosophy, but only read life at first hand." I am aware that such statements can be disingenuous and self-excusing, so I went on to read great slabs of the book to determine what I thought of him in depth. But I found I could relate comfortably to his perspective.

He said that you have to learn how to appeal to your own intuitive judgement and be able to speak with impudence (!), merely in the hope that there will be kindred souls who will agree with you. He also talked about becoming friends with the authors you discover: "friends in spirit". He is not merely talking about his contemporaries, he is likewise referring to writers going back over hundreds and thousands of years. I liked that. He said he had learned to treasure their select company, and also that of "greater ones" who are present "more as masters than as companions of the spirit". He gives Chuang Tse as an example: someone whose serenity of understanding is effortless and completely natural.

Like Lin Yutang, my sources are eclectic: random and eclectic. I generally fail the academic test of having read the right authorities. He comments that "there is greater pleasure in picking up a small pearl in an ash-can than in looking at a large one in a jeweller's window". A book fair is very much like Lin Yutang's ash-can.

The title of the book, *The Importance of Living*, seems to be ironic, or a conundrum. What is it about? I am bearing in mind that it was written just prior to the Second World War. And I am also bearing in mind that there is little patience today for anything deemed to be "old". "How could it be relevant to us these days?" Or, perhaps the book was made irrelevant by the war. Could it be deemed to be naïve?

Yes, of course. Or, perhaps. Or, perhaps not. Lin Yutang is wrestling with great themes. One epigraph at the front of book is from Confucius: "It is not truth that makes man great, but man that makes truth great." The other epigraph is also pertinent today, when a popular theme of books is how to do nothing, as a counterpoint for the stress we accumulate when we move too fast, and incessantly, without pause for rest. Chuang Ch'ao: "Only those who take leisurely what the people of the world are busy about can be busy about what the people of the world take leisurely."

There are fourteen sections in the book. They include:

- Views of mankind
- Our animal heritage
- On being human
- Who can best enjoy life?
- The importance of loafing
- The enjoyment of nature
- The enjoyment of culture
- The art of thinking.

As Van Loon does in *The Story of Mankind*, Lin Yutang comments on the imperfections of our systems of government, yet he says, for all that, we have to accept our place as humans. Ants might be more rational and better-disciplined, but do they have museums or libraries? But, we should recognise that much of our progress arises out of playful curiosity, not seriousness. There is the element of mischief and fumbling in those who delve in science, technology and cultural avenues. They experiment; they make mistakes. We need to accommodate this in our visions of government and order.

I was intrigued enough about Lin Yutang to look up a biography of him. It is difficult for me to write a short summary of his life because it was so interesting, and full of surprises. He was born in China in 1895 and went to university in Shanghai, afterwards going to America to study for a doctoral degree at Harvard. He became a teacher and writer, but had wide interests, including Chinese politics, and he also invented a typewriter that produced Chinese characters. He was brought up Christian, but in adult life he studied Chinese religions – Confucianism, Buddhism and Taoism.

In 1933, he met Pearl Buck, the American author, in Shanghai, and she introduced him and his writings to her New York publisher. After 1935 he lived mainly in the United States, although he lived in China and Singapore for several years after the Second World War. He wrote extensively about Chinese philosophy, way of life, art and culture. He wrote over thirty-five books in English and over fifteen in Chinese. His works are said to represent an attempt to bridge the cultural gap between the East and the West. He lived the last years of his life in Taiwan, dying there in 1976. His major books have remained in print.

I find much of Lin Yutang's observations about life still quite pertinent, not to be brushed aside in a rush. But holding his book, a nicely produced hardback, I admit that part of my interest is in wondering what it would take for me to be prepared to produce one of my own books in hardback. I have written over twenty books, but the only one I have produced in hardback is *They Went to Australia*, which is a picturesque book about the voyages on which all of my direct ancestors came to Australia from the British Isles (between 1838 and 1860). It will unquestionably stand the test of time.

I think that for me to produce a hardback book, I would have to think that the book would continue to be pertinent, even significant, after a long period of time. I find it manageable enough now to write a book and issue it in paperback form and then turn it into an ebook. I think well enough of my work that it is acceptable for it to be reproduced in those forms, but a hardback is more daunting.

However, I have the teasing thought that one day I might write a book that is worthy and appropriate to be produced in such form. So, it was worth buying a second copy of Lin Yutang's book, one that had not been vandalised.

The inside covers, back and front, have a watercolour picture of a group of Chinese folk lounging by a lake with mountains in the distance. Two of the six are playing musical instruments, and the others are listening, a classical portrayal of luxuriously doing nothing without any expenditure of money.

I can't tell you what the book cost when it was sold, because it is not pencilled on the inside cover, but I can tell you that it was sold at ELL's, The Book Centre at Newcastle. It has a little sticker to say so. The vandalised copy doesn't have this information.

Final score for the book fair = 3.

## 4    Brookvale Lifeline Book Fair

(Friday 7 July 2023)

The next book fair I went to was at Brookvale. I hadn't been to this book fair before. I found fourteen books that I already owned, so the score for this book fair was fourteen. But wait! It wasn't quite that simple. I was slightly off in respect of two of those books. As it happened, two of the books were actually other books by the same author. I thought I had *The Art of Happiness* by the Dalai Lama, but I didn't. Instead, I had another of his books: *Ancient Wisdom, Modern World: Ethics for the New Millennium.* The other instance was with Graham Hancock. I found *Fingerprints of the Gods*, but the book I owned was *Magicians of the Gods*.

This unanticipated state of affairs reminded me of the scoring in Australian Rules. If you kick the ball through the centre pair of posts, it is a goal and you score six points. If you kick the ball through either of the side pair of posts, it is called a behind, and you score one. When they tell you the score in Australian Rules, they tell you the whole thing: like "four goals and seven behinds", and then the total score (which would be thirty-one in this case).

So, to adapt this artifice, I will amend my score for Brookvale to "twelve books and two authors"! I am not going to introduce the complication of assigning six points to each book. Let's do without that!

I was wondering why fourteen books would turn up, when at Galston, the score had been just three. Was that a random thing (remembering that coincidence is another word for "we don't really know why"), or did it relate to the kinds of books that crop up in different suburbs? Or was this increase prompted by my greater attention to the idea? It could have been the latter; of course it could.

I am aware that most people don't think about such things. That doesn't mean I shouldn't.

## 4. The Secret
By Rhonda Byrne

The first book I found at Brookvale that I already owned was *The Secret*. And I wondered, is there something about why this book turned up now? Perhaps I should be interested in it again. Perhaps they relate to things I have been thinking about at the moment, or things I could be thinking about - in a new context, or with fresh understanding.

I have to say that, when I got home, I searched through my library to find the books that I already owned. (For the pedantic, I kept track of the books by taking photos of the covers on my phone.) Out of all the books, *The Secret* was the only one I couldn't find.

This happens; people visit me and borrow a book, or I lend it, and I seldom see it again. This is fine; it is in the nature of books to keep circulating if people feel some attraction to them. That's ironic, because the main subject of the book is the "law of attraction". One hopes that the vagabond books are appreciated by those who acquire them.

*The Secret* appeared in 2006 and was hugely popular in the United States and Australia (and probably in other places too). Many people are still enthusiastic about the book, for example: "It has absolutely changed my perspective on life" and "It's always a good reminder to keep me on track for manifestation."

When I read it, I felt the need for a breath of caution. I had known someone who sought to manifest a red sports car. She felt that the universe owed it to her, and she would have it if she just focused on it. If this was the message, I thought it was somewhat inappropriate. The book would have served only to cement a person in self-absorption, whereas spirituality is more about finding peace and healing through contentment and service to others. There is a great stream of religion in the world today that aligns spirituality with wealth: the "prosperity gospel". It is very popular.

To be stern, I think books are only helpful if you are also attuned to the potential harm that can (will) ensue if you allow their message to override things you know to be true. You have to bring a high set of values with you. I read Bishop Spong's book, *The Sins of Scripture,* many years ago. He said you can't read the Old Testament, and read about the slaughtering of people deemed to be bad, and think it is okay to slaughter people because you read it in the Bible.

Spong said, you have to bring your values with you, and use them as a filter. You are responsible for your values. By the sins of scripture, Spong means "those terrible texts that have been quoted throughout Christian history to justify behaviour that is today universally recognised as evil". Likewise, we can't read a new book and allow it to justify a moral misdirection such as selfishness, and unseemly attachment to materiality.

I am loathe to criticise books, because people can get helpful or needful messages in places that did not attract me, but I also have to stand by my own counsel. And some books pass through and are interesting for a time, but then their flaws become evident.

There are other books that delve into the "secret" of manifestation. Often, the emphasis is on health and well-being, that is, on how to deal with the advent of sickness or disease. Deepak Chopra is one; I discovered one of his books at the book fair too. My assessment: definitely worth reading. And another is Herbert Benson's *Timeless Healing* (1996), which I found at a previous book fair. My assessment: definitely worth reading. A more recent book is Joe Dispenza, *Becoming Supernatural*, which some people might find helpful. I don't use the word "supernatural" myself unless I am talking about a category of fiction. Again, not to disparage; people find help in places where others don't.

"Each our own way we must go the desert, where the angels will minister to us." (me)

My quest has pushed me back into my library. I am glad I have a library, which is to say, I am glad I keep books. In the memoir I wrote recently, *Long Time Approaching*, I talked about how I started gathering books in my late teens. Of course, at that age, one does not really have plans. Well, I don't have plans now either, but I do have the intention to keep and maintain my library, which means I keep my eye open for books that would be worthy additions to my scope of interests.

## 5. You Can Heal Your Life

By Louise Hay

This was the first time I had been to a book fair with the mission of looking out for books that I already possessed. It put a different slant on the book fair experience. It meant that I was attuned to books that I had had an encounter with, even if that encounter had been ten or more years ago. Even if my thinking had developed or changed direction since then. Or, the principles in the book are so much a part of my thinking now that I don't even think about them consciously. Or some bizarre and totally human mixture of all the above.

Louise Hay's book, *You Can Heal Your Life*, fell into that category. Some people would say it's just weird New Age stuff. The harsher critics might say it's a threat, because it undermines our recourse to appropriate treatments by the mainstream medical profession. I would say that the point of books is to raise issues up and put them in your face (about thirty centimetres away, namely, reading distance) and ask you to give them consideration, especially if you've never thought about those ideas before.

I have also found that this new quest of mine is forcing me to dive in again and give the books fresh consideration. And that's what a library does; it means that all those sometime-quests are always still nearby. After the first excitement of discovery, reading the book the first time, the book continues to be present in the sober light of day, always asking you, at least potentially, how you reconcile it against the light of everything else in life.

I realise that this topic teeters on the edge of much bigger questions. You could ask: So, Glenn, what books did you buy? And how do they relate to the books you already own? And these are good questions. My interests have changed over time. Over the last twelve months, I have become interested in books that are about books themselves, and even books about writers.

At the moment, I would merely say that at the latest book fair, I bought a book called *Reading the Seasons*, by Germaine Leece and Sonya Tsakalakis (2021), and I mention it because they quote a passage about books (by Samuel Crother, "The Literary Clinic", *The Atlantic*, September 1916). Crother says, "There is nothing so harmless as printed matter when it is left to itself. It lies there without power of motion. It can't follow you about. It can't buttonhole you and say, 'one word more'. When you shut up a book it stays shut."

But although that may be literally(!) true, the books still lie there waiting. Another writer, Stefan Zweig (1881-1942, Austrian and Jewish, famous in Europe in the 1920s and 1930s) said this of books: "The books are there, waiting and silent. They neither urge, nor press their claims. Mutely they are arranged along the wall. If you direct your glances their way or move your hands over them, they do not call out to you in supplication. They wait until you are receptive to them; only then do they open up. First there has to be quiet about us, peace within us; then we are ready for them. As you sink down into them you experience repose and contemplation, a relaxed floating in their melody in a world beyond this world." (from his biography by Geoge Prochnik)

The allure of books awaits our response, like Lin Yutang. What is *The Importance of Living* about? And Louise Hay awaits my response once again. *You Can Heal Your Life* was first published in 1984. My copy is the tenth printing from 1987. It is very tattered and dog-eared. I don't know where it came from, but I have had it a long time. The book has been around so long that one of its phrases – "You are worth it" – has been appropriated by advertising agencies for their own purposes.

It's a delicate balance to apprehend the correct spirit of a message without becoming waylaid into less worthy by-roads where selfishness holds sway. There is a healthy aspect to the message, "You deserve to be a success in every area of your life", and there is a misguided interpretation. Unfortunately, the lower interpretation is the one that is more attractive, but that way lies delusion. On the other hand, there is little that is helpful (or healthy) about pessimism, and there is such a thing as living in a victim state. To work though these things and become mature is the work of self-cultivation.

Today, I heard a story about a man who committed suicide. It was a difficult circumstance, because he had been a teacher of meditation, so it seemed inexplicable. A while ago, I heard the story of a Reiki master who committed suicide. The lady who told me had been a follower of his, and the event caused her great distress. Didn't this undermine everything? Don't these two events indicate that everything written in books like Louise Hay's is wrong, misguided, and even dangerous?

It occurs to me that Stefan Zweig also committed suicide. So here we are: when you open a book, you let a lot of things in, and then all of life rushes at you and asks for an answer. Everyone lives in their own circumstances and with their own mental furniture. Obviously, as these three examples show, this means that even a person who has cultivated growth can be overwhelmed. I read Stefan Zweig's biography; I have some inkling about why he committed suicide. He was a Jewish man who lived through the 1930s and watched Hitler take over Germany, and then Austria, proceeding to crush the idea of civilisation that Zweig held dear.

However, it is over-reach to say that a book that offers a transformation in one's way of life is wrong because of such an event. The meditation teacher and the Reiki Master had not resolved all of their personal demons. It doesn't mean that meditation and Reiki are false. The message for me is not to depend too much on 'gurus'. The message for other people might be different.

It is said that when Mark David Chapman, the killer of John Lennon, was found, he had a copy of *Catcher in the Rye* in his hand, and that this therefore made J.D. Salinger and all of his books suspect. I would consider that to be over-reach.

"In the infinity of life where I am, all is perfect, whole and complete." This statement occurs over and over in Louise Hay's book, followed by particular messages: I see any resistance patterns within me only as something else to release; I am one with the Power that created me; I live in harmony and balance with everyone I know. But what if this is not the case? Does one cultivate a form of schizophrenia by repeating these sayings? Is this what happened to the meditation teacher, for example?

These are not easy questions. Eventually you have to face it all and dig deep. What can you say that is meaningful, and not trite? And I end up looking around at my entire library for help. But I have tried at various times to articulate something helpful. At the end of my latest book (2023), *Long time Approaching*, I put it this way:

"First, be contented. Then, use all of your capacities to make the most of your life: your intelligence, make peace with your emotions, and be awake to what is happening around you in the present moment. Always be ready for transformation."

Of course, that's not enough. Nothing anyone says could be enough, but there is the concept of growing up, the idea that we may start our lives living in shadow and ignorance, driven by fears and hunger, but we can evolve beyond that. We can become aware of life as a gift, which begins when we trust that all is perfect, whole and complete. This is what I mean by contentment. And we may have to remind ourselves of this continually. And occasionally we feel life as bliss, we see beyond our small self, we see ourselves as part of something bigger, and then we can live in harmony, whatever difficulties our day-to-day lives present us with.

Therefore, I value my battered copy of Louise Hay's book. She wrote other books after that. I don't think it matters where you come into the room, as long as you look for something that will help you grow into a better person. You can filter out things that you find too hard. The point of a journey is to keep walking along the path. Perhaps the book could have said more about the ego, although I appreciate that when one writes a book, one is focused on a particular question or questions, and does not want to get diluted by trying to answer everything.

My perspective is that more needs to be said about the ego. For a start, you need to "be careful what you wish for". King Midas wished that everything he touched would turn to gold. His wish came true, and he quickly realised that it was a rash wish, driven by selfishness. But then, this message wasn't what readers wanted to hear. Nevertheless, it is the ego that tempts us with material goals and unworthy acts to obtain success. It is important to talk about that. There are other books....

"I am not bound to win, but I am bound to be true." Abraham Lincoln said that.

Did I have anything in particular in mind when I read the book? Not really. I was interested in the ideas, and whether they offered an illuminating perspective on life. However, I had had asthma as a child, and it had always been a scary experience. I had also felt helpless, and at some points, if I had had the power, I would have considered not even trying to take the next breath.

By the time I was a teenager, asthma showed up mostly before exams. The irony was that, by this time, I was getting high marks, and coming top of the class in most subjects. There was no reason for me to feel nervous about exams. There was a particular episode when I was fifteen where I felt the attack coming on, and there was an exam that day. Previously I would have succumbed and stayed home, but this time I was suddenly angry with myself. I said, "This is ridiculous! You are fully capable of doing this exam. There is nothing to worry about. Go to school." Note, it was me telling myself this, not my mother or anyone else. It was my decision.

I went to school, sat the exam, did well, and I never had asthma again after that. People say, "He grew out of it", meaning the asthma, but my version of it is a little bit different. I made a personal resolution, and I believe that that's what made the difference. And I don't care if other people scorn my point of view.

So, did Louise Hay say anything about asthma? She did. She said asthma represents "Smother love, resulting in an inability to breathe for oneself. Feeling stifled. Suppressed crying." Was I the recipient of smother love? Arguably. However, I accept my own responsibility in this. Bruce Lipton (see below) says that our environment affects us in the way we take shape, but he also says it is more subtle than that; it is about how we perceive our environment. Two people may react to the same environment in different ways. Accordingly, I would say that my reaction to my family circumstances was to feel smothered – none of this conscious, of course. Then, when I was fifteen, I was finally ready to burst out of the shroud I was under.

I found Louise Hay's depiction of this trigger for asthma persuasive. Overall, however, I felt that one could be too formulaic about this approach. One needs to treat it as potentially insightful information against the whole tapestry of one's context. It's interesting that the books of Deepak Chopra and Bruce Lipton turned up at the same book fair.

## 6. Ageless Body, Timeless Mind

By Deepak Chopra

This book was published in 1993. I heard someone say recently, with a touch of cynicism, that he looked older now (2023, thirty years later). Yes, he does, but he looks very much alive. He was born in 1946, so he is just four years older than me. I feel I have a good measure of what 'old' can look like when you are chronologically into your seventies. He looks okay to me. I feel kind of okay too.

Out of interest, because you know I am interested in the life of books, the book was originally purchased at Gleebooks in Sydney in November 1993. The receipt is still in the book. I bought it 10-15 years ago at a book fair. It is priced: two dollars. A good bargain.

Sometimes I buy books because people are talking about them, and I want to know what the book says. The person who bought the book before me was interested too. The first half of the book is underlined with key quotes. I'm not sure if he/she finished the book. The second part of the book is more about exercises and practices to undertake. Maybe they did that, or maybe they were satisfied with what they learned early on.

Did I take the book seriously? Did I read it or take up any of the practices? Am I ageless?

I know I didn't read all of the book at the time. From memory, I was reading a similar book: *The Biology of Belief* by Bruce Lipton. I will write about that later, because I also saw that book at the book fair. Also, I purchased (new) Deepak Chopra's earlier book, *Quantum Healing*, and read all of it assiduously. I bought the 2015 edition; it had originally been released in 1989.

What are some of the things the previous owner highlighted in *Ageless Body, Timeless Mind?* "The unseen world is the real world." "There is incredible liberation in realising that you can change your world – including your body – simply by changing your perception." "A lifetime of unconscious living leads to numerous deteriorations (heart, digestion, hormone regulation), while a lifetime of conscious participation prevents them."

"Our essential nature is a flow of intelligence." Chopra talks about the role of the mind in the placebo effect. He discusses the role of conscious intention in enabling us to remain youthful. I liked this quote (which was underlined): "You have to want to rejoin the flow of the body before you can learn from it, and that means you must be willing to open yourself to knowledge that was overlooked in your old way of seeing."

Chopra quotes the ancient Indian sage, Shankara: "People grow old and die because they see others grow old and die." Anticipating my reading of Bruce Lipton, Chopra says, "Belief creates biology. Life is awareness in action." In the body of the book, Chopra discusses the mystery of aging: negative factors that lead to aging, and positive factors that retard aging. He encourages readers to move away from social, collective beliefs about the nature of life, and move towards personal realisations.

These start with the idea that "I am Spirit" rather than merely flesh and blood. The other realisations are: "This moment is as it should be; uncertainty is part of the overall order of things; change is infused with non-change; entropy holds no threat because it is under the control of infinite organising power."

I think that these statements need the context that Chopra provides, if one is to understand them. He charts the shape of a life that opens up to timelessness rather than one's consciousness being time-bound, if that makes sense. He ends with poetry, quoting the Rig Veda: "Although my spirit may wander the four corners of the earth, let it come back to me again so that I may live and journey here." His conclusion is that people don't grow old; when they stop growing, then they become old. I think there is much wisdom in that.

There is a new book from Deepak Chopra (2023): *Living in the Light*. It arrived with the courier this morning. I haven't read it yet, but I can say it is a tastefully produced hardback, giving the impression of white. The first half is about yoga: the big picture, Raja Yoga, and the second half is by a compatriot, Sarah Platt-Finger, and it is about yoga as a set of asanas (postures).

It raises the question of time. Do we have time to read all these books? Frankly, none of us does, given the wealth of books we live in the midst of. I say two things: "This moment is as it should be", and "First, be contented. Then, use all of your capacities to make the most of your life."

There is also a further question: have I digested all that I have read? Do I even remember all that I have read? So, it is not a speed contest to read all the books; there is this further question. My library has a lot of books in it. I don't claim to have read them all. But of the books I have read, do I recall them? From the perspective of distance, was it worth reading them?

I don't feel the need to recall everything. However, often a book affects the way I see the world. This will become evident with the next book, *The Biology of Belief.* There is always work to do to digest a book. Perhaps you need to underline passages the way the previous owner of my copy of *Ageless Body, Timeless Mind* did. Perhaps you need to write something down, or carry out a practice. Perhaps you need to contemplate an idea deeply, perhaps you need to feel an incident in the book in your heart.

Often the central idea of a book will seep in slowly over time and become a deep part of your life. In that way, it will change you. You find that you use it in your life, and it figures in your conversation. You refine it and make it your own. Living is learning.

## 7. The Biology of Belief

By Bruce Lipton

The idea that our perceptions (which are affected by our beliefs) affect our body came to Lipton with a shock. He was a cellular biologist, and had worked on the assumption (that is, the belief) that the life course of a cell was determined solely by its genetics. He began to see that this was a misreading of events. In fact, the cell's life course was largely determined by its environment, and by its perception of its environment. For a single cell, its awareness is largely reflexive, but for humans, who are so much more complex, our response to the environment is much more a matter of choice. We are not victims of either our genes or our environment.

The field of epigenetics has grown out of this realisation. The activity of our genes is constantly being modified in response to life experiences. This is in contrast to the idea that genes 'control' our trajectory in life, for example, by making us susceptible to this or that disease. Our beliefs can be self-limiting. Cells respond to our thoughts and beliefs. Lipton asserts that a shift to a sense of empowerment over our own life can lead us to a richer and more satisfying life.

The Human Genome Project commenced in 1990 and was completed in 2004. My own prediction at the time was that the focus on this project would push the emphasis onto genes as the cause of diseases. The old "nature versus nurture debate" would be swamped by scientific findings of links between genes and disease. My prediction was that after this excitement had abated, emphasis would come back to the environment as a precursor to diseases, and our interaction with the environment. In other words, we would not be seen as passive victims of the environment either.

Lipton says "We are made in the image of God, and we need to put Spirit back into the equation when we want to improve our physical and mental health." He admits that this assertion makes him seem crazy to many people. I would say we need to be open to the fulness of life, and over time this changes us for the better. It is not healthy to believe in the traditional Darwinian approach to life – the survival of the fittest, the necessity for competitiveness. Lipton offers us the science that supports this perspective. It is no longer outlandish.

What I took away from *The Biology of Belief* was the simple but profound idea that life is governed by a trinity of factors: genetics, environment and consciousness. There is more to life than Nature and Nurture. In the book, Lipton takes the reader through his moments of insight, sharing the excitement of his shifts in perceptions and beliefs. What was attractive to me was to see how science is not simply a flat compendium of facts that compel given conclusions. Rather, it is a set of constructs that ensue from, and are ultimately limited by, a given framework of beliefs. Remember, we used to believe that the atom was the smallest thing in the world?

Ample evidence supported the idea that the earth was the centre of the universe. Copernicus presented his conclusions based on a different set of observations; some of these observations had been available but had been routinely ignored because they did not fit the existing belief structure. In his modern examples from cellular biology, Lipton was showing that this is still the case: findings that do not fit with existing ideas are ignored. In fact, this is always the case. Wasn't it Einstein who said "Imagination is more important than knowledge"? And this statement is trotted out happily because it is glib and seemingly profound, but if you realise that it is indeed really true, it is not glib at all but revolutionary, a form of enlightenment.

Lipton takes the reader through his discovery of quantum physics, and how it opened his eyes to a world beyond Newtonian physics, one that enabled sober consideration of medical phenomena such as healing, and the benefits of acupuncture, chiropractics, prayer and meditation. The universe is now seen as a flow of information (energy), and it flows in every direction, all at once. The linear-causal, material model of life is succeeded, and the concept of life as an energy field, where the mind is a key player, is acknowledged.

To pursue the idea that the mind is a key player in our lives, we need to consider the power of placebos and nocebos, where neutral substances or practices can result in positive or negative health outcomes. Lipton ends his book by explaining how his study of cells over a lifetime has turned him into a spiritual person. His belief became that our essence is spiritual, and his point is that this belief grew out of his scientific discoveries. It was not a result of a "leap of faith". Moreover, he has applied these beliefs in his own life and he attests to their power. He attributes this to the reconciliation of science (biology) with quantum physics. Everything is imbued with spirit.

It has been several years since I first read this book, but it has been reaffirming to read it again. This time I was also able to relate it to Deepak Chopra's books, which I did not have the advantage of doing before.

## 8. The Four Agreements: Companion Volume
By Don Miguel Ruiz

I am interested in the connections between thinkers and how they connect with each other's work. Ruiz is Mexican, so I wondered whether he was associated with Carlos Castaneda. I had come across the latter a long time ago, I guess in the 1970s. He was a cult figure, I suppose, among New Age people. There was an air of danger about him. He might offer you power, but there was a risk of harm as well in his methods.

Here is a passage from Castaneda's book, *The Teachings of Don Juan*: "Don Juan seemed to want me to work with the devil's weed as much as possible. This stand was incongruous with his alleged dislike of the power. He explained himself by saying that the time when I had to smoke again was near, and by then I ought to have developed a better knowledge of the power of the devil's weed."

I had read that passage a long time ago too. I had seen people tripped out on drugs, and I thought that playing with drugs as a pathway to power was fraught with "foreseeable risk". I didn't think that spirituality had much to do with the wish to acquire any kind of worldly powers. I was more attuned to the path of discipline and practice. Examples would be yoga practitioners and meditators. Monks as well, although I was not interested in sequestering myself from the world. Even church-goers, although I had ended my association with churches.

I should note, too, that in 1969, Charles Manson had instigated the murders of seven people in California, including the actress Sharon Tate, in two crazed knife attacks. The murders were carried out by three teenage girls who were members of Manson's 'family'. Lots of LSD was involved in the life of that maniacal group. I had some respect for LSD, but it was obvious that it could be used for evil in misguided hands.

However, I was prepared to believe that what Castaneda was talking about was "beyond my ken". It was just that there were many paths up the mountain, and I wasn't going to follow all of them. At the same time, I was interested in what I could learn from other traditions, so that left Don Miguel Ruiz as an open question. Several people had told me that they thought his book was good, whatever that might mean.

I finally bought the book when I was browsing in a bookshop that I don't normally frequent, W.H. Smith's. It wasn't so much a question of being prepared to spend the money, it was a question of being prepared to spend the time to read it. It was a small book, so it was within my capacity. There had been a book called *The Four Agreements*. The book I bought was called the Companion Book: "Using the four agreements to master the dream of your life". I wasn't thrilled about mastering the dream of my life, but I thought, "Ah well, that's probably just marketing." The publisher was Amber-Allen Publishing at San Rafael in California. The book was published in 2000.

Ruiz turned out to be a healer, born 1952, descended from an ancestral line of healers in Mexico, called Toltec. I had heard of Toltec through Jon Anderson of the progressive rock group Yes. He had released an album in 2007 that delved into Toltec wisdom, part of Native American traditions. This was a poetic approach. He sang about the wisdom of the earth, and care of the planet, so I felt that I was on wholesome ground. Ruiz had studied medicine and become a surgeon, but he returned to studying the ancient wisdom as a young man.

The Four Agreements are simple, even starkly simple. They are:

1. Be impeccable with your word.
2. Don't take anything personally.
3. Don't make assumptions.
4. Always do your best.

These are agreements you make with yourself. Ruiz maintains that following these four agreements will transform your life. Each of the rules requires explanation, which he does in the book. There is a set of beliefs behind them, an understanding about the nature of the world and our part in it. The first agreement is to resolve to live in integrity, which reflects largely on how we use words. Don't tell lies or deceive others, and don't criticise or gossip. And keep your word; your words and actions should be consistent.

The second rule is about judging others, and also about judging yourself. Humans tend to live as victims. We are brought up that way. He calls it getting domesticated into our family's and society's culture.

The third rule is about accepting uncertainty in life. We usually assume that we know things, but very often we are mistaken. We have to ask questions and be open to the real answers, and also accept when we don't really know.

All the rules are demanding of us. The fourth rule shows this clearly. We must live the best life we are capable of. But we will be living for ourselves, not the lives other people desire of us. We will not be living up to social expectations, or the image of ourselves we have created from what we believe other people want of us. He says we can learn how to heal our emotional body and be fully alive.

In following the four agreements, one learns mastery and freedom. One also learns to be clear-minded, and be able to transform energy. "Then every action we take is an expression of the One Being."

He explores the role of perfection in our childhood: "Our image of perfection is the reason we reject ourselves; it is why we don't accept ourselves the way we are, and why we don't accept others the way they are."

He addresses many queries that people have in seeking to apply his teachings. What if you are still facing challenges in life? He says "If you don't have challenges, how do you know if you are evolving? It's your action-reaction that makes the difference."

What if you have always thought you are lacking in some way? Is it just a matter of telling yourself the opposite? He says our beliefs are stored in our mind with our agreement, and we have practised this all our life, so it is automatic. Our reasoning mind can say something else, but it is lying. We have to replace the belief with another belief, and actively practise the new belief. Practice results in mastery.

I think that Don Miguel Ruiz's teachings mesh with the teachings of others such as Deepak Chopra and Bruce Lipton. At one time I was writing commentary on management in organisations, and I spoke with a consultant who had had a dramatic experience with an organisation through using just the first of Ruiz's agreements.

The organisation was having trouble with its internal climate: people were not getting on well and the atmosphere was chronically aggravated and full of blame. The consultant's prescription was that everyone spend a month being "impeccable with their word" to each other. It meant, for example, that if you scheduled a meeting for 10 AM, you would be there at 10 AM; you wouldn't be late and then say you were really busy or something had come up, and imply that you could do this because you were an important person. It covered everything you said at work. You wouldn't be loose about it. You would keep promises, and you wouldn't make promises if you knew you couldn't keep them.

The difference it made in one month was extraordinary. Above all, relationships between everyone improved markedly, including between levels of management. Morale had soared, to the amazement of all the employees. The consultant called it "the integrity principle".

I think Ruiz's tenets are challenging. They are about being honest with yourself with no excuses and no ego. Then they are about trusting yourself and your place in the universe – your right to be here, and not as a victim. Do I compare books – "This one is better" etc? No. We all find our way to various books, and individually we find them more or less useful.

After reading *The Four Agreements*, you realise you are responsible for your actions and reactions. Living well is about practice;

awareness and deepening practice. I think this is a book that is certainly worth coming back to periodically.

## 9. Wisdom: Peace

By Andrew Zuckerman

This book was easy to buy. It promised a look at the concept of wisdom, it was small (155 mm square) and attractive – hardback, with coloured photos. It consisted of short interviews with thirty-five famous people on the subject of wisdom, with the sub-text of peace. The interviewees were all over sixty-five years of age. They came from politics, music, theatre and other professions, such as architecture. They came from all over the world, including Australia.

The book therefore presented a wide assortment of experiences and perspectives; it wasn't a theoretical treatise on wisdom. What would I do with such a book? I would skip through it and pick out certain people at random and read what they had to say. I would keep it on my bedside table for a while and read segments before I went to sleep. I would ponder what the idea of peace meant to them, and how that affected my own ideas about wisdom.

The book was the concept of Andrew Zuckerman, an American photographer and movie maker, and it was supported by Archbishop Desmond Tutu. As well as being a book, it was a film and a travelling exhibition. But it's not easy to talk about wisdom. The word can so easily be applied in a trite way, so that it is merely a gesture of approval. What does it really mean?

As is my wont in such situations, I started with the dictionary. *The Shorter Oxford English Dictionary* says it is the capacity of judging rightly in matters relating to life and conduct, or soundness of judgement in human affairs. To call someone wise is to consider them worthy of dignity and respect. They may have a deep knowledge of a particular subject. Sometimes a wise person is treated as the contrast to a fool. All of these meanings can be pushed into the shape of a particular religion or dogma, or it can be left very broad. It can be seen as ancient wisdom and it may be allied with magic.

I think that wisdom can be considered in a practical way, so it is virtually a synonym for 'astute', but it may also be considered in a more spiritual way, referring to a person who has a deep understanding of life in its largest sense. I have a number of books on wisdom, and they are very different to each other. I haven't studied them yet, but I suspect that they may pursue conflicting perceptions of wisdom. Then there are the books that don't even mention the word, but are seeking to present an illuminating and helpful perspective on life. After reading such a book, you may consider it to be wise.

In Zuckerman's book, wisdom is a broad umbrella. You could say it is what a number of people say, people who have had wide experience and about whom it would generally be accepted that they are not 'bad' people, when they are asked to talk about what they think about life in the world today. What would be the most helpful things to say to a wide audience, thinking of the future? What do they really believe?

Jane Goodall, the lady who worked with gorillas, began by saying, "It's awfully sad that with our clever brains, capable of taking us to the moon and developing all these sophisticated ways of communicating around the planet, that we seem to have lost wisdom." She describes wisdom by referring to indigenous peoples, who would make a major decision based on how the decision would affect people seven generations ahead. In contrast, we make decisions based on the bottom line and in short-term time frames. We are stealing our children's future.

Goodall says we are not so separate from the rest of the animal kingdom. We need to respect other species. She makes a practical suggestion: she suggests that we spend time learning and thinking about the consequences of the choices we make each day.

Graham Nash, who was part of the music group Crosby, Stills, Nash and Young, said his perspective is informed by the fact we are spinning around on a ball of mud in space, and if we all ceased to exist, the world would go on. So, in that sense we are unimportant. But on the other hand, we need to like ourselves and love those around us. And we need to recognise that there is a great deal of violence in the world and "it is completely unholy". We need to try to live our lives in peace and harmony.

Jimmy Little, the Australian Aboriginal singer, had a simple message: Remember that the most important words in life are 'Please' and "Thank you". This rule should govern all your relationships with other people.

Kris Kristofferson, another singer (American), said political change may help, but the most important change is at the directly personal and emotional level, where we feel a connection with every other human being.

A British actress, Vanessa Redgrave, spoke about the importance of human rights, the sadness of governments that violate human rights, and the readiness of people to accept governments that violate human rights.

Yoko Ono, John Lennon's widow, said the most important things in life are simple, like breathing and imagining peace. When you are doing that, you can't kill somebody or abuse them. You become an oasis of peace. When we say, "We are all one, it is true: yes, we are all one."

Desmond Tutu said, "We can each be an oasis of peace. We can think good thoughts, and the ripples from that flow out around us and touch others."

Yes, the mix of people talking about peace is a wild assortment, but it shows that everyone relates to peace, and wants it for the world and for themselves. It's good to be reminded. And as small as we each are, it is evident they all believe that peace must start with each of us as an individual.

### 10. The Art of Happiness: A Handbook for Living

By The Dalai Lama

Sometimes I can be slightly off the mark. It seems that I don't own *The Art of Happiness*. However, I do have a small collection of books by The Dalai Lama. I understand why I don't have the book on happiness. I don't think this is the main issue in human life, despite it being portrayed as such by many people. It doesn't help that a country, the United States of America, has in its Declaration of Independence, the statement that humans "are endowed by their Creator with certain unalienable Rights, that among these are Life, Liberty and the pursuit of Happiness".

I think it is not just one thing that we want. It is more helpful to point to four things, a small collection of aims that provide their own balance. They are Competence, Morality, Beauty and Love. I know you could go on from there and name a myriad of things, but I think this collection is sufficient for most purposes, and certainly more helpful than just saying we all want to be happy. This raw statement probably needs context. I first set out this idea in my book, *Long Time Approaching* (2023). The context is there.

In the context of the four aims I identify, happiness seems too vague, but I admit, it is also a matter of the perspective that you bring. In my small collection of books by The Dalai Lama is a book called *Ancient Wisdom, Modern World: Ethics for the New Millennium*. I bought this because I wanted to find out what he had to say about ethics. (Yes, I was writing a book on ethics.) Ironically, for me, he introduces the topic by saying we all wish for happiness. He clarifies that statement by saying it expresses our wish to avoid suffering.

He compares rich, developed countries with poor, undeveloped countries, and comments that the rich are not happier than the poor. He puts this down to well-off people focusing more on external factors – the accoutrements of wealth. Their external abundance is accompanied by inner suffering (for example, anxiety, isolation, depression). It is not just money, but other factors, such as urbanisation, pervasive technology, lack of reliance on each other, and rhetoric that drives incessant growth and development, that fuel unhappiness.

When The Dalai Lama discusses ethics, he defines it as actions that do not harm others' experience or expectation of happiness. But to fully appreciate the role of happiness in ethics, we have to realise that humans have the capacity to experience deeper levels of happiness, not merely satisfaction of the senses. Understanding this means that if we only view the material aspects of life, we will miss this deeper meaning.

The Dalai Lama says that the principal characteristic of happiness is peace, an inner peace that is rooted in concern for others and sensitivity to their condition. The sustaining of a healthy ethics in a society depends on us retaining "our regard for others' feelings at a simple human level". We call it compassion. Our aim ought to be the transformation of our minds and hearts so that we are spontaneously ethical, seeking virtue in our daily lives. Then he brings the argument to the idea that happiness arises from virtuous causes.

"If we desire to be happy, there is no other way to proceed but by way of virtue." A generous heart and wholesome actions led to greater peace. Peace and happiness are allied.

Do I still want to pursue my construction of Competence, Morality, Beauty and Love? Yes, I do. The idea arose when I was engrossed in studying my family's history. In all the various strands, on my mother's side and my father's side, they were predominantly tradespeople: miners, engineers, painters, stonemasons, carpenters. The women were likewise competent, as wives, mothers, and often as dressmakers as well. So, they all worked with their hands to earn a living. What could I say that was specifically relevant and helpful to them?

It is our capacity, and honour, to grow up and learn how to do things that are useful in the world, so that, as modest humans, we can hold our own. We make families and households, we bring up our own children, and we participate in our communities. At a base level, we stand on our own feet financially. All of this falls under the umbrella of competence, but it also calls in the other qualities.

When I think of Competence, Morality, Beauty and Love, I think of how all my predecessors, my ancestors, survived and looked after their families and brought their children up to likewise make their way in the world. And they did this, certainly for the most part, honourably. I suspect most of them enjoyed the happiness that comes with inner peace that is acquired through virtuous conduct.

I suspect I will write more about this. I feel informed by The Dalai Lama's perspective.

## 11. A Little History of the World
By E.H. Gombrich

When I first started reading as a child, I found it magical. There were whole worlds out there, and they were as close as the covers of a book. I went on journeys then, great journeys to places I had no idea existed. And to ideas as well. Then I would go to sleep and wonder how it all fitted with my idea of what the world was, and who I was myself in that evolving world. A book about the history of the world makes that child-wonder explicit!

E.H. Gombrich's *A Little History of the World* was not a childhood memory for me – it was not available in English in the 1950s – but it was written for children. I found the book at a book fair when I was researching for my book *Future*. I don't like saying I was researching, because I was just thinking about an idea, and these books started turning up, so I started buying them and reading them. My ideas kept taking shape. It was always possible that I would sit down and try to put them into book form. It depended on the people I met. I mean that in the sense that Lin Yutang meant it. The people you meet in books may become "friends in spirit" and "companions of the spirit". I was dipping into ash-cans and picking up gems.

In fact, the urge to write *Future* grew as I discovered more, and wondered about the perspectives of the people who write histories of the world. I eventually sat down and put my ideas together. Some of it was more about the questions that remain rather than the answers I had established.

Gombrich's book was a gem. It cost me five dollars at a book fair in about 2018. I loved what it said on the inside front flap: "In 1935, with a doctorate in art history and no prospect of a job, the twenty-six-year-old Ernst Gombrich was invited to attempt a history of the world for younger readers. Amazingly, he completed the task in an intense six weeks." It was published (in German) and released in Vienna to immediate success. Unfortunately, it was soon banned by the Nazis, for its pacifism!

I discuss his book in *Future*. I commented that he didn't write the book from a base line of ignorance. He had a scholarly background in art history and so had a good sense of historical context. And I suppose it was only natural that the book should also be published as an illustrated edition.

After the banning of his book, Gombrich realised that the rising Nazi dominance was dangerous, and with his new wife he fled to London. He stayed in England during the war, working for the government, but he returned to Austria when the war ended. However, he maintained his connections with Britain, and continued his work at the University of London. He received numerous honours, including a knighthood in 1972. He revised his book on the history of the world and eventually translated it into English in the 1990s when he was in his eighties, but it was not available until 2005, as *A Little History of the World*.

There are forty chapters in the book, starting with the early stages of the planet, before there was life, and then talking about the predecessors to humans. He talks about ancient civilisations, the genesis of the major religions, the rise of empires and cities, the age of discovery from the 1500s onwards, and the rise of nations and of colonies, and the events of the last two hundred years. There is much wonder in his approach, as is appropriate for a story to be read by children.

No one would deny there is much to consider in the history of humans. One might be interested in the development of technology, or wars, or our difficulties in combatting climate change, but the broad canvas on which these problems occur is the history of the world. If one is not intending to be a history scholar (and Gombrich is not claiming that his book would replace history textbooks), the book is inviting. In accepting Gombrich as a "friend in spirit", I had to agree that optimism is important. The nuances one might deem necessary would arise in the conversations about the book that you might have.

But I have not told you everything. As well as this book, there is an illustrated version, first produced in 2011. I did not realise this until I went to a book fair and found it. I realised what it was: a copy of the book I had, but with nearly every page illustrated with coloured pictures. It was beautiful. I was excited. The version I obtained was the paperback version, produced in 2013. And the version I found at the most recent book fair was again the illustrated paperback version. No, I didn't buy a second copy. I felt that I didn't need it. I was satisfied.

## 12. The Signature of all Things
By Elizabeth Gilbert

It is odd that Elizabeth Gilbert's book is in this list. At the book fair, I had the thought: Will I include fiction books? I decided 'No.' I thought that if I extended my scope that far I would lose all focus. But I did look in the Fiction section. Most of it was not of interest to me. I think most fiction books are comfort stories. They may shock you in parts, but you are confident that it will all be sorted out by the last page, much as you feel confident in watching a horror movie. It might titillate, but it will not undermine your world view.

Moreover, you know the stories are made up, and the author could have changed any of the elements of the story anywhere along the way. The interest is in the imagination of the author, and the illusions he/she is able to create. It's like watching dancers on stage and being delighted by the moves they make. Or like a group of children around a campfire, saying to an adult, "Tell us a story."

I have written some fiction, but not a lot. And I do read fiction as well as 'thinking' books. I am drawn in by books that deal with deep themes and are plausible. There is the thought that this could have happened to you or someone you know. This year I have read *The Garden of Evening Mists* by Tan Twan Eng, about a Japanese gardener in post-World War Two Malaysia. I read *Children of the New Forest* by Captain Frederick Marryat, first published in 1847, about a group of children whose family was loyal to King Charles I during the time of the English Civil War, in 1647. I gained an insight into the politics of the time and the social structures, and the momentous decisions that the orphaned children had to make.

I also read *The Word for World is Forest*, by Ursula Le Guin, whose work I love (fantasy or science fiction). And *The Law of Dreams* by Peter Behrens. All of these books affected me emotionally. They made me look at specific people and situations and consider the issues they were wrestling with. It all feeds back into the ideas I have about all the different aspects of reality – justice, power, hierarchies, nature, growth, change – everything! And my feelings about it. It goes back to my initial excitement about reading, that from a safe place I could explore the wonder and horror of the world, and consider how to live in it, how to live well.

So, reading Elizabeth Gilbert's book, a work of fiction, was not really an aberration. And the book had such an effect on me that I recognised it immediately at the book fair. It is a large novel, almost 600 pages, with an exquisite cast of characters and vast themes. The lead character, Alma Whittaker, is a botanist who studies mosses, and she is introduced to the ideas of evolution. She was born in 1800 and encounters Charles Darwin's theory of evolution, and studies mosses in relation to that theory. But also, she has a lover who is an artist who draws orchids, and he is a follower of Jacob Boehme. Boehme was a sixteenth-century German mystic who believed that every life form has its own unique signature that captures its essence – the "signature of all things".

There is a tension between these different perspectives: the traditional religious views about life created by God, and the new, scientific ideas that examined life in terms of its measurable causes and effects. And beyond that, the mystical perspective on life. I appreciated Gilbert's depiction of this struggle, but the magical moment for me was when Alma was examining her mosses and realised that evolution was happening right then, right in front of her, in the adaptation of each moss to its immediate environment. Here was the manifestation of "survival of the fittest".

To fully appreciate my realisation, you must understand that I had always thought of evolution as something involving vast sweeps of time, something that happened over millions of years, not something that was happening here and now. I know this is silly, but something can be in front of you the whole time and you don't see it until a certain moment. Perhaps the light falls a certain way and you suddenly notice it differently, as if for the first time. My view shifted from the events of millions of years to the events of this moment in time.

That was how I felt while reading about Alma Whittaker studying her mosses. So, was it later that I read Bruce Lipton's book? I am not sure, but the two experiences are now woven together. It means that I understand evolution as being alive at every moment, so it is important to understand the nature of the process, as Alma sought to do. The key phrase is "the adaptation of an organism to its environment", not "the survival of the fittest". The latter points us towards battle and conquest, while the former indicates awareness, intelligence, responsiveness and innovation. There is an intellectual contest of nearly two hundred years wrapped up in these two expressions.

Then I come to a question I have not mentioned before: in what category should I lodge Elizabeth Gilbert's book? Fiction? Or should I keep it alongside the likes of Bruce Lipton and Deepak Chopra? Categorisation is one of my unrealised goals. I have a rough system, with a nod to Dewey, but it is imperfect and it is creaking. In the case of *The Signature of All Things*, the decision was not difficult. I forewent the Fiction category and placed it with the other books about the big story of humankind. My final criterion is "Which category is most helpful to me?" Easy.

## 13. A Short History of Nearly Everything
By Bill Bryson

Before I go onto the next book, I have to discuss categories in more depth. The question has come up with an impending seriousness because my bookshelves are getting crowded. At the same time, there are a few empty shelves. Obviously, I could solve this problem if I re-organised deftly. I thought maybe I needed more shelf space for some categories, but I have been avoiding this issue. The logical part of my mind says that if I understood everything in life in depth, I could determine the appropriate categories readily.

Fortunately, I have not gone down this path. I believe it would have been depressing, and ultimately a failure. Logic alone will not sort this problem out, much as the logical brain would like to think it could. Part of the problem is that I do not have infinite shelf space. It has a limit, even though my garage library has many shelves, and even boasts an aisle, and even though my library extends into several rooms of the house, and down the hallway. Another issue (although not a problem) is that my library is not infinite either, and I do not want it to be. My library is an expression of my interests. It is not a library for all of society, democratically or universally. The more nuanced statement is that my library is a history of my interests over time.

I started reorganising books with the idea of creating breathing room. I took a crowded shelf and identified one topic within it: Ecology and Climate Change. I rehoused those books on an empty shelf. Then I viewed the books on the now less-crowded shelf; the topic was the history of humans and the world, and I reordered the books so they would be more comfortable. The older books went together, for example, Gombrich and Van Loon. (There is also a book called *The Adventure of Mankind*, by Eugen Georg, which is a first edition in English, published in New York, 1931, translated from the German. I found it in a Lifeline bookshop (not a book fair) and it cost me six dollars. It belongs in this section. I found the same book online for US$600.)

I started a new section, 'Biography', and I found three books I could move from their present positions to there. Some of my categories are only temporary. I am thinking of writing a book on choosing careers, so I have grouped some books together with that in mind. They went from a stack (always a sign of losing control; stacks should only ever be very temporary) to a new space.

All in all, I worked for a morning and finished up with most shelves having some space for new books: breathing space. Sometimes I move things around, and this is one of the reasons to have some empty space on the shelves. For example, I realised it would make sense to have all the books by The Dalai Lama together, so now they are. And I found numerous books with 'wisdom' in the title, and I think that's interesting, so I put them together. Is the word 'wisdom' just used cheaply, thinking it will sell more books? Or is there something of substance tucked away in there? And are there some very different things masquerading under this one name?

I feel better. I am breathing more easily. I can feel the increased scope created by the work I just did.

What is *A Short History of Nearly Everything* by Bill Bryson doing in my library? And in fact, it turned up twice. When I was working on the book *Future*, one of my daughters suggested to me that it might be helpful in giving me some context. So, I bought it, and then later, she gave me a copy of it. I gave one copy away to Lifeline, but I still had a copy of it and I might not even keep that. And I found it again at the book fair. Perhaps I would read it and then pass it on.

I was reading a wide assortment of books with the book *Future* in mind. I had always thought that Bill Bryson only wrote travel books, so I didn't immediately see his relevance to me. Belatedly, I realise that that was only his starting point, and he has now written about a vast array of subjects. Obviously a man who thinks deeply about everything!

I remembered the book at the book fair because of the recommendation from my daughter. I bought it because… Well, I didn't need to. That was odd, wasn't it? But there is always Lifeline. Books flow to and fro. Matthew Battles, who wrote a book called *Library*, said that libraries breathe in and out, as if they were alive.

Bryson's book is 600 pages long, and I read it all. It certainly served as background thinking for *Future*, so much so that it didn't make into the book's bibliography. It is called a rough guide to science, or a layman's introduction. His perspective seemed to be that science is made up of ordinary people who determinedly and innovatively try to understand the world around them, and explain it to others. I think Bill Bryson's core talent is as a mediator of knowledge.

I can appreciate his work. I spent many years working for a publishing company that produced commentary on management and particular areas of management, such as human resources, work health and safety, and employment law. So, I saw my role as doing just that – mediating law and academic knowledge to working professionals. I thought it was a worthwhile and not insignificant skill. In reading Bryson's book, I was also appreciating the work that he was doing as a mediator of knowledge.

I learned a lot about the history of humanity from the perspective of science. This was different to looking at histories of humanity, because the subject matter there is power, government, business, religion, technology, social conditions, economic systems. Science gave another context for the story of humans, based on the physical conditions of our lives. It was grounding to read this.

However, Bryson's book is very much about people. When he is talking about the big changes to our planet, for example, he talks about the scientists involved in noticing oddities about their environment, and where their curiosity led them. He talks about their surmises in the light of the knowledge of their day, and the contest of arguments in the academic sphere. He talks about those who were wrong as well as those who were right, especially those who were right in a prescient way, long before their ideas were accepted.

An Australian Uniting Church minister, the Reverend Richard Evans, is part of the show. In his spare time he searches the sky for supernovae: giant stars that suddenly collapse and explode, releasing in an instant the energy of a hundred billion suns. Evans says if that happened anywhere within 500 light years of us, we would be annihilated. When a supernova occurs, the effects are seen just for a month or so. Finding supernovae is an exceptional talent, not the province of an automatic program running on a giant telescope.

Bryson mentions that the term supernova was first coined in the 1930s by an irascible Bulgarian at a Californian observatory. He was brilliant but not a good communicator, so his ideas were often brushed aside. Yet, his conception of the supernova and neutron stars proposed the occurrence of events that would be the largest in the universe, and which would explain phenomena that baffled astronomers. He also proposed the existence of dark matter, which explains how the universe coheres gravitationally.

In this way, scientific knowledge seems to continually refine its ideas. In the geological world, it most often proceeds by providing viable explanations for phenomena that were formerly unexplained. And Bryson points out where anomalies still exist. Our ideas about the movement of tectonic plates includes evidence from biology. Certain types of plants occur in various places around the world and this indicates where those places were located millions of years ago. Thus we can conclude that the tectonic plates moved in certain directions at certain times. But even now, not all of this information is consistent with the theories we have proposed. We cleave to the theories in the interim.

Knowledge is always in flow, and we have to accept its provisional nature. Bryson recognises this, and realises that it is not always a popular position to take. His perspective also recognises that our existence is subject to sudden termination. For all our cleverness, an asteroid could hit the earth without warning and end all life on earth. Yet we continue to survive, and it seems a fair assumption to make that we will continue to do so.

Bryson delves into the story of DNA, which was first discovered in the 1860s by Johann Friedrich Miescher, but he did not know its purpose. He thought that it might be the agent of heredity, but the idea did not attract any attention at the time. It was thought that DNA was too simple to perform that purpose. The question was still a mystery in the 1930s. Bryson tells the story as a play of personalities, some of whom were brusque and some of whom were retiring and tended to be overlooked. He recounts the troubles that Rosalind Franklin had as a woman in a traditionally male environment, being treated patronisingly despite her invaluable contributions to the quest.

The current picture of the nature of life seems impossibly complicated, but there is also an underlying simplicity, and a unity in the way life works, across all forms of life, from bacteria to humans and other animals. We are even closely related to fruit and vegetables. At the end of his book, Bryson says, "As far as we can tell, we are the best there is. We may be all there is. It's an unnerving thought that we may be the living universe's supreme achievement and its worst nightmare simultaneously."

It is tempting to view science and its accomplishments as a tide of progress, where it is only a matter of time before we know, and understand, everything. But Bryson does not appear to see it this way. He recognises the greater complexity that is evident every time we break down another barrier in particular spheres. For example, we have mapped the human genome, but around 97% of DNA is inexplicable and seemingly useless. We have the gall to call it "junk DNA". We simply do not know what it does or how it is activated.

Bryson notes that we have not yet been able to create life, much as we have experimented. And he notes that we have not yet fathomed the link between the mind and the brain. Through neuroscience it would seem that there is a connection, but the focus of science as it is currently practised is on material phenomena, not on mental phenomena or consciousness. The latter are widely seen merely as peripheral.

## 14. Fingerprints of the Gods

By Graham Hancock

It seems appropriate to go from Bill Bryson to a book that treats of other phenomena that are inexplicable. I was introduced to Graham Hancock when I was working on the ideas for *Future*. It was suggested to me that I should read *Magicians of the Gods* (2015), so I bought it and read it (another big book: almost 600 pages). The book that I found at the book fair was not the same one. Graham Hancock has written many books. I found *Fingerprints of the Gods* (1995). I bought it.

The connection with Bill Bryson is the idea that the pursuit of science is surrounded with the mythology of objectivity, the idea that all scientists are objective and they are not swayed by personal opinions, beliefs and biases. Bryson showed that this is often not true. There are prevailing ideas at any given time, and scientists adhere to them as closely as any other group in society that is harnessed to a raft of accepted notions. Evidence to the contrary is dismissed out of hand. This is the norm for human behaviour, even that of scientists.

What I ended up writing in *Future* is as follows:

> It is a modern conceit to think that all of the old artefacts (pyramids, stone circles, ancient writings etc) are conveying myths only. It is a predisposition, even an ideology, rather than appropriate objectivity. The intention, it seems to me, is to avoid having to think about the possibility of any of the accounts being true in any sense. It fits with our idea of ourselves as the greatest and most knowledgeable generation in the history of humanity. The irony is that some of the accounts talk about knowledge that was lost in cataclysms.

> Likewise we have become blasé about the extent of what we don't know. How were the pyramids of Egypt built? Or the giant structures in Baalbek, Lebanon? Or the stone circles at Gobekli Tepe? Or the Mayan pyramids? Or the stone circle at Stonehenge? Or the Inca structures at Machu Picchu? Or the Angkor Wat temple in Cambodia?

> Why are so many of these structures carefully aligned with the cardinal directions (North, South etc) and with constellations of stars? Some of these orientations suggest intimate knowledge of the movement of stars over a span of thousands of years.

> Some humility is called for. I am no scientist or archaeologist and I have no bold claims to make. I do not believe in magic or aliens. These are children's concepts, just like the arguments that say God is dead and we have only the laws of physics to keep us company.

I do believe that things make sense, but only when your mind is open and willing to consider things that might upset your current concepts of the world.

Once upon a time, most people believed that the Earth was the centre of the universe, and the sun and planets revolved around the Earth. I think that if most people today had grown up believing this, Copernicus would not convince them otherwise. Copernicus might present his evidence, but then someone with a loud mouth and an intemperate amount of scorn would say it was nonsense, and we would go back to the barbecue, unchanged. Collectively, we are as bad as we have ever been.

Even if this were not so, it is hard to keep up with new knowledge. Frequently we hear a story from a scientist or historian that "changes everything we thought we knew about…." But the textbooks and websites are seldom being rewritten fast enough to reflect these changes. (pp. 118-119)

There is more, but I will leave it there for now. I suppose some people disparage Hancock because he is not a member of an academic institution. He is an independent investigator, a former journalist. Yet I find his work credible. And as Bryson points out, new ideas in the sciences can be shocking to accepted understandings.

It is now accepted that a giant comet struck the earth around 12,000 years ago, a cataclysmic affair that abruptly changed the climate and caused the worldwide extinction of many species of animals. Hancock argues, not that this event was responsible for the development of civilisations, or that it instigated the rise of civilisations, but that it disrupted existing civilisations that were far older than we have imagined, and sophisticated in both technology and outlook. He suggests that hunters and gathers picked up on the skills of these earlier civilisations.

This is a very different view of our past, and it challenges our idea of ourselves as the clever people who arose out of the crude lives of hunters and gatherers. Hancock offers this idea after surveying evidence from ruins around the world. He sees these as the fingerprints of an ancient civilisation that may have rivalled our own knowledge.

In his newer book, Hancock says that it does not overthrow the hypotheses put forward in the earlier book. Rather, the new book builds on its foundation.

I find his ideas worth entertaining (which is different from saying his ideas are entertaining!). We ought to accept that we do not understand how the monumental structures in those ancient places were built, or how they achieved the accuracy they did. And it makes sense for someone to consider the possibility that ancient myths are not all merely fanciful, just tall stories around the campfire.

I suppose it doesn't help that Graham Hancock's book titles are outlandish: fingerprints of the gods, magicians of the gods. One assumes they were dreamed up by the publisher. Yet, as I said, I find his work credible, methodical and thorough, and he certainly engages in ongoing conversations with professional geologists and other scientists. He has a sober, meticulous mind, one capable of seeing connections between disparate things. It is worth asking, what if he is on the right track?

It would mean that we have more deference for past peoples. It would mean that we accept our vulnerability on the earth: we are not invincible, and we could be wiped out, either by a space object colliding with us, or by the cumulative effect of our abuse of the environment, particularly over the last few hundred years. It means we would ask, seriously, if we could live with reverence for the environment, and how this could occur? Would an enlightened leader or leaders enable us to achieve it?

The question I raised in *Future* was whether we would do anything individually, or whether we would resign ourselves to the helpless choice of wishing for a magical leader or government to fulfil the next beautiful plan. It doesn't do to concentrate on this matter without relief.

## 15. London Lives: Poverty, Crime and the Making of a Modern City, 1690-1800

By Tim Hitchcock and Robert Shoemaker

It was interesting that Hitchcock and Shoemaker's book on London in the 1700s appeared at the book fair. I am constantly delving into my family history; there is always something to be discovered or solved, always some issue to clarify, always another person in the family tree to be unearthed. When I first started this work, I was solely focused on immediate facts – persons' names, dates of births, deaths and marriages, places where they lived. However, when I had something that looked like a family tree, I started to wonder about the social contexts in which these people had lived.

Accordingly, I started to read books and stories about the social contexts. I suppose the convicts' lives attracted me first, because their lives were so stark, and so often miserable. There are three convicts in my family tree: one is my mother's great grandfather, William Archer, and the other two were a couple (married in Hobart), my father's great grandparents: Edward Lewis and Sarah Crosby. I am sure that neither my mother nor my father knew that they had convicts for ancestors.

Gradually I started venturing further. I became interested in the broader social patterns of the times. *London Lives* turned up on a table outside a bookshop, on sale, although it was only recent (2015), and I bought the book because I thought I might tackle it eventually. (My library has many books that I haven't read yet, but I will read one day. That's how I think it should be.)

The book is a little early for my purposes. William Archer was born in 1813 and was convicted in 1838 at Harpenden, north of London. Edward Lewis was born in 1829 and was convicted at Middlesex General Sessions (north London) in 1845, and Sarah Crosby was born in 1833 and was convicted at the Old Bailey in 1849. Yet, the book did provide a broad landscape for London life as the city was developing in the century leading up to their misadventures. Certainly, poverty and desperation were the inescapable factors in their lives.

The book *London Lives* is one result of an extensive study that focused on the poorer people of London in the eighteenth century, along with thieves, prostitutes and highwaymen. It examined large masses of records, and the book works in conjunction with a website and database of names of people of the time. The authors say the information shows how poor people managed to survive in difficult circumstances, and in their "acts of desperation, the poor and the criminal exercised a profound and effective form of agency that changed the system itself".

Once I had introduced myself to the website, I became tantalised. I started looking up names. I knew that William Archer's parents were Edward Archer and Mary Clifton. I knew that Edward Lewis's parents were William Lewis and Mary Everitt. Sarah's parents were Irish, so they were not relevant. Most of the records I found were too early to make any direct connections.

But, it was tantalising. For example, in the records of the Carpenters' Company, in 1723, William Lewis was declared bound to John Manuell for seven years. I assume that this was not one of my ancestors, because the location was in Nottingham, not Bethnal Green (northern London), where Edward's father lived. However, Edward's father was a cabinetmaker, which is related to carpentry. It seems clear that the Carpenter's Company is a guild of tradesmen and that William Lewis is signing up for an apprenticeship. Further, the record states that William Lewis's father was William Lewis, pointing to the tradition of a son being named after his father. So, one gets the idea that there is a tangle of threads in the database, and some of them will be connected to people in my family tree.

One of the realisations that the book brought was that people in my family were present during momentous periods of history. When I started exploring family history, it seemed to occur in its own little bubble of births, deaths, marriages and migrations that was quite separate to the events that occurred in the history textbooks. But if Edward Lewis was born in 1829, and he was the fifth child, his father William Lewis was probably born around 1800, and his father in the 1770s. In 1788, the First Fleet left London for Botany Bay to establish a new penal colony. My Edward Lewis was to follow one day, as a child convict.

The transportation of convicts to America had ceased in 1775 following the declaration of war by the American colonies. Crime in London was chronically high, and the population of the prisons began to increase inexorably. Prisoners began to be housed in hulks on the River Thames, a system which was worse than the prisons, and led to malnutrition and disease as overcrowding grew. In 1777, over a quarter of the prisoners died, and public outrage was growing.

There were numerous escapes, some of them of groups of prisoners, and a feeling of resistance was brewing in the community. In June 1780 a public riot broke out, continuing for almost a week. Over 285 people died, and public buildings were attacked and burnt, including Newgate prison, which was not in operation again until 1784. The causes were multiple, but the focus quickly became policing and punishment.

In the aftermath, the authors say prisoners tended to be more resistant to their gaolers. They were desperate but defiant, and they argued and planned new strategies for self-preservation. Then, the French Revolution in 1789 added to the wariness of authorities about being too harsh on the poor, while likewise tempting them to crack down on disruptive behaviour.

It was this volatile atmosphere in which my great great grandparents grew up. In 1838, William Archer was arrested for stealing twenty-eight pairs of "high shoes"; in 1845, Edward Lewis was arrested for pick-pocketing ten shillings from a lady at Kensington; and in 1849, Sarah Crosby was arrested for stabbing a policeman in the arm after she was refused entry to a Refuge for the Houseless Poor on a winter's night.

My family shared the fortunes assigned to the poor. In critical moments they rose up into the public eye: with bravado, desperation and defiance. Their London lives became Australian lives, treading new paths, with optimism outwearing the grind.

### 16. The Meaning of Tingo
By Adam Jacot de Boinod

Occasionally, in among the welter of topics that engage my interest, there are books about words themselves. *Tingo* is a book of occasionals, if you like. It is not a book that lends itself to being read systematically, but one you pick up occasionally and read snippets. My copy is special in the sense that it has a dedication at the front: someone gave it to me. I also happen to have a newspaper article on the book, published when the book was published. I think the book was given to me soon after its publication, so the article coincided with that time.

The article pointed to the book's quirkiness, featuring foreign words for concepts for which there is little or no parallel in English. 'Tingo', for example, is from the Easter Islands; it means to borrow objects from a friend's house, one by one, until there is nothing left. Given the size of my library, I should be wary of tingo!

It's a very funny book, because you invariably think that the concept is possible, even though it may seem strange. It gives you a different perspective on everyday life and the people you might come across.

De Boinot said that his venture started one day when he picked up an Albanian/English dictionary and found that there were twenty-seven words in Albanian for moustache, and a similar number for eyebrows. He found that other languages have different words for things we might regard as universal, for example, we say that cats go 'meow', but in Mexico they go 'tiatzomia'. But mostly the book is about concepts we would regard as unusual. 'Serein' is a word for rain that falls from a cloudless sky – in French. 'Torschlusspanick' is German for the fear of diminishing opportunity as one grows older.

'Dokidoki' is Japanese for rapidly pounding heartbeats caused by worry or surprise. 'Ongkang-ongkang' is Indonesian for sitting in a relaxed fashion with one leg dangling down. The Indonesians have another double-word for when the head bobs up and down with drowsiness: 'teklak-tekluk'.

Some concepts we may be familiar with, but another language has just the right word for it. If something is not too much and not too little, it is 'lagom' in Swedish: just right. Our expression 'so so' is mirrored in other languages: 'cosi cosi' in Italian, 'hai hao' in Mandarin, 'azoy azoy' in Yiddish, and 'thik thik' in Gujarati (Indian).

The Japanese have the expression 'Ichigo-ichie', which is the practice of treasuring each moment and trying to make it perfect. 'Mubshar' is Persian for being exhilarated with good news, while 'ai bu shishou' is Chinese for being so delighted with something that you can hardly take your eyes off it. 'Sekaseka' is to laugh without reason in Bemba, Congo and Zambia.

De Boinot notes that the Japanese have an exquisite vocabulary for the deep joy that comes as a response to beauty: 'uttori', to be enraptured by the loveliness of something; 'yoin', the reverberating sensation after the initial stimulus has ceased, and 'yugen', an awareness of the universe that triggers feelings too deep for words.

The result of this perusing is not so much an expanded vocabulary as an improved appreciation for the range of human experience across different cultures. There is, of course, a section on the many words for snow in the Inuit language. There is also a section on

Scottish words for their damp climate, such as 'dreich' for a miserable wet day, and 'plowtery' for showery days, which may turn to 'gandiegow' (squally).

*Tingo* lives in my category for language, which includes books about writing. It comes out from time to time, perhaps on days that are 'dreich' and I just wish to be 'ongkang-ongkang'. On those days it is 'lagom'.

## 17. The Alcohol Experiment
By Annie Grace

I generally describe the books I write as falling into four broad categories: reflections on experience, ethics and values, family history, and poetry. However, the books one acquires fall into a much wider range. Annie Grace's book came about because I was assisting a person to get started on writing a book. The book was about boundaries, more particularly, the boundaries that people working in mental health roles should set for themselves to avoid burnout.

It was about boundaries in your relationships, and boundaries with yourself. It was primarily focused on work relationships, but it recognised that the value of this work extends to personal relationships as well. The core of the book was to be a program of self-training, supposing you accepted that you needed to put the ideas into practice and change personal habits, not just read a book. The book didn't get completed at the time – other events intervened – but Annie Grace was suggested as a good person to exemplify the design of a program of self-training.

Also, the idea of experimenting with quitting alcohol is relevant to many people who are feeling overwhelmed with their caring and support roles. Many carers rely on alcohol to get them through a day, or the week. Annie Grace's book provided the outline for a 30-day challenge: don't drink alcohol for a period of thirty days, and use that period to think about the habit and whether this could be the start of freeing yourself from the habit.

The person writing the book suggested that I read Annie's book to gain a perspective on the type of program we were trying to design. Coincidently, I had recently quit alcohol. I felt that I was drinking too regularly. I could persuade myself that I was not drinking to excess, but I realised that my usage had increased over the previous few months rather than remaining steady or decreasing. And I thought that to play with it by telling myself I would decrease, for example, by having x days per week alcohol-free, would not be productive.

So, one day I just quit. Curiously, it was the beginning of "Dry July", when people take it on as a collective challenge to stop drinking alcohol for one month. They support each other and make a public declaration of their intention. The idea seems to be to break the pattern of drinking and to establish the counterpoint of a period of time without wine or beer or spirits. And it is a period of one month, or one cycle of the phases of the moon.

However, I didn't want to be part of any social bravado. And I didn't want to create any dependency on a group of people trying to do the same thing or coaching others on their 'progress'. The error was mine: I had lazily fallen into the pleasant habit of having a drink or two of wine every night. And I could not deny the fact that, after the second drink, the third always became more attractive. I had to think about what my reasons were for having the second or third drink, or not having it.

I read Annie Grace's book and I found it worthwhile. She systematically digs into the reasons we give ourselves for a given path of conduct, that is, a given set of habits: it's nice; it's not doing me any harm; other people do it. And there are endless social supports for this barrage of reasons – what people do in movies and are forgiven for (say, he/she has had a hard day or something bad happened), what advertisements say and project, in the nicest possible way, what commentators say and assume in their commentary (even the fact that interviewers have a glass of wine on the table). It is a consolidated picture that supports drinking at every turn.

I was not acting out of any need to proscribe what other people should do. We are all at different points in our journey. I just wanted to get it clear for me. I had one hiccup in my venture: drinking socially. After several months, I thought that I would like to drink with friends on a festive occasion. I wanted to see what that would be like. Unfortunately, it was Christmas at my place, and it went over several hours, so I did not have the means to stop at a certain point, and I drank too much.

Afterwards, I thought it through, and I decided I shouldn't do that. It would be better to say at the start, to others: "I am not drinking." Again, if I had to create a limit, the best limit to set was at the beginning. There was no point in having "one or two drinks". I had to establish at the outset what I was going to drink.

Now I come to another aspect of my venture. In Annie Grace's book there was, I thought, a flaw. She seemed to be of the opinion that the idea that wine could taste nice was a lie. She seemed to be saying that in fact it all tasted awful – wine, beer, you name it – and people just lied to each other about that, everyone deluding themselves. I took exception to this idea. I felt that hundreds of years, even thousands of years of experience said otherwise. The drinking of wine (for example) crosses many countries and cultures. It is fair to say that the making of wine is part of established civilisation, or high culture. The occupation of sommelier would be entirely a fraud if this were not true.

I felt that it did the "no drink" argument no good to claim that all alcoholic drinks tasted bad. Fortunately, my new path coincided with the advent of non-alcoholic wine and beer in the market. Suddenly they were a very public and growing part of popular consumption.

I thought this was important, because what I really enjoyed was sitting down at night and having a glass of wine. And, I enjoyed having a beer after an afternoon working in the garden. And I quickly realised that the drink did not need to be alcoholic. So, I discovered a wide range of wines and beers that I could drink happily. It meant that I could retain the habit of having a "refreshing beverage" without drinking any alcohol. One of the interesting aspects of this was that some of those wines I did not like, and some of them I did. That was enough in itself to reject the idea that all wine tastes bad – some of it does, and some of it tastes quite good.

The next mountain pass was deeper. All this time I was continuing to ask myself what it was about alcohol that attracts a person. Sure, people drink heavily because they want to lose awareness and control. They are in search of oblivion; they don't want to be responsible for a while, usually because there is something bad in their life that hurts.

But, on a couple of occasions when I had an alcoholic drink (I had not taken a vow the way some people do, and I wasn't going to beat myself up if I had an alcoholic drink socially), I started to notice the very moment when the alcohol takes effect. It didn't need to be very much, but there was a moment when the alcohol arrived in my bloodstream. I could notice that very moment.

So, I wondered what was it in that moment, and where did it lead to? I realised that what I wanted to recover, perhaps from fifty years ago in my life when I was on the verge of adulthood, was the sense of living without that kick. Would I be joyless if I lived without it? Could I relax and be happy without any of the stimulation that alcohol gives? On this point, I think Annie Grace had worthwhile things to say. She talked about how people use the 'relaxation' argument, but tend to descend into abandon and lack of awareness.

Then, when I was on Christmas holidays (the following year), my daughter asked me if I would accompany her to a winery for a wine-tasting, as she wanted to buy some wine. I was driving, so I wouldn't have been drinking much in any case. The revolution was that she suggested that I just have a tiny taste, and she would drink the rest. I liked this suggestion. So, I had just a taste of each wine – there were six – and she drank the rest. When I got to the sixth wine, I finally felt it, the feel of the alcohol in my system. It was just a tiny thing, but it enabled me to ask, what was I looking for when I used to drink? And can I live without it?

I can live without it, because all the time I have not been drinking, I have been thinking about who I am when I am not drinking, and thinking: "That is okay; that is the real me. It is good, it is aware, it is healthy." And I was thinking, "Do I need alcohol in order to enjoy myself?" Surely, enjoyment has to be in enjoying who I am, and enjoying the essence of the moment?

I am not arguing against alcohol altogether, but I did need to get out of an entrenched habit. I have a store of personal admonitions. For example, "To get out of old habits, persevere." Personal admonitions are useful if you have a suitable context for them. They should not represent harshness or a way of life that you do not see as admirable or sustainable. They should be assertions you are happy to live up to. My context is that of a wise person who lives gently, firmly and clearly. I believe it is worthwhile to live that way.

Such a person enjoys life simply and sincerely. One expression for this way of living (from old Chinese literature) is "a jug of wine and two bowls of rice when the sun goes down." So, I accept that a wise person may on occasion enjoy "a jug of wine". But you have to establish your inner basis first, or I might say, re-establish it.

So, then I wondered what the book was doing at a book fair. Did someone buy the book but then give up on the experiment? Did they disagree with its arguments or its approach? Or had they followed the path and obtained their value from it, and were now passing it on to others for their benefit? We don't know, do we? But we can hope for the best option. I did not buy the book, because I already had a copy, and I left the copy at the book fair for someone else to discover and explore.

This is the way of books, to flow between people and encourage self-cultivation.

## 18. Book Acquisitions

That is end of my list of books I saw at the Brookvale book fair that were books I already owned. They were popping up out of the past: my recent past, my intermediate past and my distant past. It raises the question: do I keep buying books on the same topics, or do my interests evolve? The answer to that would lie in a list of the books I bought. I did buy books, didn't I, despite the fact that I haven't read all of my books yet, and despite the fact that my shelves are already well-populated?

Yes, I did buy books, but my first observation is that taking note of the books I already owned made the whole process harder. It was distracting to stop and take a photo of the covers of the already-owned books. Usually I make a quick mental note and move on quickly, focused on what is new and interesting. I have an analogy for this. In the field of learning theory, there is the concept of the "zone of proximal development", developed by Lev Vygotsky, a Soviet psychologist, in the 1930s, but only translated into English in 1978.

This zone is the space where learning occurs; it is at the edge of a person's knowledge. If you are focused on learning something new, it is where your attention concentrates. You are looking backwards and forwards and trying to fit new information to what you already know, or making a new category for it. I feel that this is what I am doing at a book fair. In a sense, it is what everyone is doing. I go to book fairs because I am looking to expand and consolidate my knowledge.

I thought about providing a list of my new books, but I won't. It's too broad for me to try to make sense of it for anyone else. The thoughts are largely unformed as yet; you could call them proto-thoughts. Sample this:

- *Philosophy in the Garden*, by Damon Young (eleven great authors and the ideas they discovered in parks, yards and pots)
- *A Spectator's Guide to Worldviews*, edited by Simon Smart

- *Where Song Began*, by Tim Low (Australian birdsongs and how they changed the world).

In their own time, the books will be opened and explored. The ideas will be churned around and moulded into evolving thoughts. As Vygotsky would say, the books will feed into a zone of proximal development, and in writing, I will expand my field of understanding.

I did buy another book, though, that has prompted my reconsideration of my library. It is simply called *Library*, by Matthew Battles. It is a history of the library in the course of civilisation. It is giving me a new perspective on my own library. I have always struggled with how to categorise it. I adopted a loose Dewey system, where topics are numbered one to a thousand. One of the shortcomings of this is that I am not interested in acquiring books in line with that classification.

For example, I am not interested in Chemistry (540) or Biology (570) as sections of books in my library. On the other hand, there was a long phase where I acquired books about Leadership, so where one library might just have '658' ("General Management") as an integer, a library that is for managers might go to three or four decimal places (for example, I acquired a 'Discarded' book from a management library, and its catalogue number was 658.408 – "Decision-making and Knowledge Management"). I have about a hundred books on leadership.

I have not yet resolved the issue of categorisation. Matthew Battles' book, *Library*, offers a few possibilities. Prior to 1500, there was one system that had three broad categories: Memory, Wisdom and Imagination. That caused me to take a deep breath. I could see the books I have written organised that way: family history and memoir under Memory, anything faintly didactic under Wisdom, which would include my books on ethics and values, and poetry under Imagination, where anything fictional would also go, if I decided to write such books.

On reflection, I thought I would do better to retain the categories I already have for the books I have written. But I still need to wrestle with how to usefully categorise all the books I own. Memory, Wisdom and Imagination don't quite fulfil my perceived requirements. But Matthew Battles has opened me up to the possibility that the system I devise could be idiosyncratic, and it could combine the features of multiple systems. There have been many different attempts by librarians over the centuries.

I can see that I will return to this topic, with it still unresolved. Perhaps my thinking will progress. For now, one of many messages I have received from *Library* is that the existence of books is twofold. First, they exist as the concept, whereby each new book contains ideas that may amuse, educate or enlighten us, and second, as a physical object which has its own individual history. As a physical object, a book makes connections across time and place, including the place where it was printed, the shop in which it was sold, and the previous owners' experiences with the book.

As Battles says: "It is the door and the key, the passport and the transport." My copy of *Library* tells me that it was owned by a lady who lived at Greenwich in Sydney, sometime subsequent to 2004, its year of publication. It is a lovely, small, gold address label. The back cover tells me that it was purchased at Abbey's Bookshop in Sydney. I wonder about what she gleaned from it, and I am happy it turned up at a book fair for me to discover.

However, one has to get back to the topic, which was....?

# 5   Books from Knox Grammar Book Fair

(Thursday 13 July 2023)

So far, I have only been to one book fair with the intention, at the outset, of identifying all the books which I already owned. I had a methodology: use my mobile phone to take a photo of the cover. When I get home, make a list, then find all of the books in my library.

The next book fair I went to was at Knox Grammar School. It is supposedly the biggest book fair in Sydney. I was still interested in finding books that were of interest to me at the moment. I had finished writing a memoir, *Long Time Approaching*, in the previous few months, which left space for new topics to be explored, added to which I still had a host of unanswered questions in my family's history. Also, the book *Future* had left many issues that begged for more to be said.

One time, I went to a book fair (at Hunters Hill) when I was in the middle of writing a book. I felt focused. I took one bag, and in the midst of a large, chatty crowd of people, I walked around purposefully, and within thirty minutes I had picked out ten books. (It was a sunny, early spring day.) I went straight back home, made a cup of coffee and started browsing through the books. They fed very fluidly into what I was writing.

For Knox Grammar, I avoided the first two hours, and when I arrived, the traders were largely finished with their hunting expeditions. Yet it was still very crowded. Parents bring their children as well. There was one book I did not find: a Sydney street directory from 1930-1940. This would be invaluable when doing family history from around that time. It means you can look up the address where a person was living, and see how close it was to certain things, and how far from the home of a significant other (or someone who was soon to become a significant other).

For example, I am currently exploring a German sailor who came to Adelaide in 1938, jumped ship, and came to Sydney in 1939. He was living at Woolloomooloo, and I could see how close his address was to the wharves. After the war was declared, he was watched by security officers, and they thought it was suspicious that he was living so close to the wharves; he could be spying and sending information back to Germany. (He definitely wasn't.)

The German married someone from my extended family. And they were put into an internment camp for the duration of the war. You can see how helpful it would be to have a street directory of the time. So, I was at the Galston book fair and I saw one! Unfortunately, it had a sticker on it to say a lady had reserved it and she was coming back for it. I even went back later to see if she had not come back, but she had, so I missed out on the book.

At Knox Grammar, I asked about old Sydney street directories, but the lady said, "Oh, we seldom see anything like that. There's not much interest in them. If we saw one, we would probably throw it out." That was painful. However, in the course of this conversation, a man nearby had been listening, and he told me about a website where I might find one. He said the website coordinated the stock of many of the second-hand book stores. I did look it up, but the oldest Sydney street directory they had was 1998. Not really close.

Did I follow through on my quest? How many books did I find? Yes, I did follow through, and it was indeed a large book fair. Fortunately, I had allowed myself a couple of hours to browse. About halfway through, I thought, "Have I bitten off more than I can chew?" Because this time, I found nineteen books. And I was amazed at the diversity of the books, both in subject matter and in time.

## A summary

| Title | Author | Year | Comment |
|---|---|---|---|
| Fields of blood | Karen Armstrong | 2014 | |
| Peoplemaking | Virginia Satir | 1972 | |
| The consolations of philosophy | Alain de Botton | 2000 | Not found; I have A |
| Dark emu | Bruce Pascoe | 2014 | |
| Sand talk | Tyson Yunkaporta | 2019 | Not found. I definitely had it. Did I lend it out? |
| Talking to my country | Stan Grant | 2016 | |
| Sagaland | Richard Fidler & Kari Gislason | 2017 | |
| Modern art and the death of a culture | H.R. Rookmaaker | 1970 | |
| The Invitation | Oriah Mountain Dreamer | 1999 | |
| The road less travelled | M. Scott Peck | 1978 | No; I have B |
| The new Chinese astrology | Suzanne White | 1993 | |
| Intuition | Paul Fenton-Smith | 2011 | I also have C |
| The element | Ken Robinson | 2009 | |
| Being mortal | Atul Gawande | 2014 | I also have D |
| 488 rules for life | Kitty Flanagan | 2019 | |
| Sydney and the bush | NSW Education Department | 1980 | |
| Sinning across Spain | Ailsa Piper | 2012 | |
| Eats, shoots and leaves | Lynne Truss | 2003 | |
| I never metaphor I didn't like | Mardy Grothe | 2008 | |

A    The pleasures and sorrows of work, 2009.

B    The different drum, 1983.

C    A secret door to the universe, 1999.

D    The checklist manifesto, 2016.

So, to apply Australian Rules scoring to the result: by my reckoning, there were 17 Books and 2 Authors. Since I found these books, I had to consider that they were being drawn to my attention. One should always consider what is being drawn to one's attention. The mind and the world interweave; it is best to seek to facilitate that flow, and see where it might lead.

Having said that, I have no argument for the order in which I have placed the books. I think it is fortuitous, although it is possible that the order generally follows the order in which I found them.

### 19. Fields of Blood

By Karen Armstrong, published 2014.

I was interested that this book surfaced at the book fair because I had looked at it only recently, and put it aside, when I was writing my book *Future* (2020). Had I been remiss and overlooked it unjustifiably? Armstrong's starting point was whether religions generally are the cause of all wars in history. Since I don't subscribe to this argument – it is facile and simplistic, more like a rant than an arguable point of view – I passed the book by.

I also wondered whether the book would turn out to be a whitewash of religions. One thinks of the Crusades in medieval times, and the Thirty Years War in the 1600s, for example. Religions were central factors in those conflicts. One also thinks of the methods of the Inquisition, the readiness to employ mindless cruelty in the cause of domination. However, it is hard to disagree with Armstrong's fundamental point, that wars cannot be understood without taking into account socio-economic and political factors. Religion may or may not be part of the mix, but it has seldom been the primary motivator.

Armstrong takes us back to the beginnings of civilisation, when humans became agriculturalists (growers of crops and keepers of livestock) rather than hunter-gatherers. With agriculture came accumulation of wealth and division of labour, which quickly led to the emergence of hierarchy and domination, supported by violence. Religions often provided a rationale for the structure of society, bringing gods, myths and rituals.

Armstrong notes that the violence was not individual or passion-based, but institutionalised and class-based. There was a dominant class and a labouring, dependent class. Moreover, religion was integrated with the functioning of society; it was not a private or personal affair off to the side. She says that the inherent problem, which we have inherited, is that this structure of inequality enabled the rise of classes of people who drove improvements in civilisation: technicians, scientists, philosophers, politicians, administrators, artists.

This fatal combination: unfairness and domination on the one hand, and social improvements on the other, seems to be with us still. It has also been responsible for developments in religion, when inspired persons have railed against the unfairness and called for a new way. Jesus's Sermon on the Mount could be taken as an example: "Blessed are the poor in spirit, for theirs is the kingdom of heaven. Blessed are the meek, for they will inherit the earth."

In India, the example Armstrong draws upon is Ashoka, who came to the throne in 268 BCE after having killed two of his brothers. Ashoka had many great victories in battle, but at some point in his life he had a realisation of the horror of war. Subsequently he devised a moral code of compassion, mercy, honesty, and consideration for all living creatures. And yet there was still the quandary of how to govern benevolently. Armstrong asserts that "Ashoka's dilemma is the very dilemma of civilisation itself. The empire, founded and maintained by violence, would paradoxically become the most effective means of keeping the peace" (p. 63).

Many years ago, I heard someone say that Jesus was misunderstood. He was not announcing a new political blueprint for the world but a personal revolution in perspective. The point of his words was that they proposed a conundrum: "If anyone slaps you on the right cheek, turn to them the other cheek also." It is hard to think of societies operating this way. It is like saying, "What is the sound of one hand clapping?" as the Zen Buddhists ask.

This person went on to say that the moment Christianity failed was when it became a success: when it became the official religion of Rome under Emperor Constantine. At this point, the church had to compromise the words of Jesus in order to maintain order among all the people who populate a society.

I think this tension is illustrated in modern times in ethical theories. There is the view of consequentialism, which says that we should judge the ethics of actions by their outcomes. This leads to the theory of utilitarianism, where the right thing to do is the act which produces "the greatest good for the greatest number of people". This theory comfortably applies in discussions of the collective good, thinking of society as a whole.

However, in the deontological point of view, championed by Immanuel Kant, morality is judged by personal factors: of doing one's duty regardless of consequences. And one's duty is "to act in such a way that one's conduct could become a universal law". What would the world be like if everyone operated this way? This approach puts the focus on personal conduct and motives, rather than the possible implications of the conduct in a given social context.

It never seems to be said in ethical discussions what these two theories represent – or that they are both apparently necessary but at the same time irreconcilable – an individual and societal perspective. Students are merely left to struggle with the contradiction. The answer seems to be "Take your pick!"

I have discussed this line of thought in my book, *A Foundation for Living Ethically* (2020), productively, I think. However, I have more to read of Karen Armstrong's book, and there are more questions that it is raising for me. Perhaps I will return to writing more based on her explorations of religions.

There is one place where Armstrong discusses the harmonisation of these perspectives, in China. Confucius evokes Kant when he says "Do not impose upon others what you yourself do not desire." Armstrong asserts that this was not simply a personal ethic but a political ideal. "If they practised *ren*, rulers would not invade another prince's territory, because they would not like this to happen to their own". But still, Confucius was "too much of a realist to imagine that human beings could ever abandon warfare" (pp. 79-80).

The Daoists, following a philosophy of *wu wei* (doing nothing), opposed any form of government. And Confucianism, despite its contribution to the education of administrators for over a thousand years, was sequestered in practice. The sentiment among the ruling class, articulated around 100 BCE, was that Confucians were impractical idealists, and were of no use in running a state.

Often, the only connection between religion and politics is martyrdom. In some modern contexts, you could say conscientious objection as well. The person holds to a point of view that the state considers to be destructive of the fundamentals of the social fabric. In one case, they offer themselves up to death. In the other, they suffer humiliation and perhaps gaol. Even modern societies find it hard to tolerate the refusal of a person to participate in its structured violence.

Perhaps I will pursue this theme. At the moment, my task is much broader: to make sense of the multiplicity of books that confronted me at the one book fair.

## 20. Peoplemaking

By Virginia Satir, published 1972.

This book goes back to my early adulthood. I bought it new ($11.45), at the Adyar Bookshop in Sydney, not long after it was released. At that stage, the Adyar Bookshop was going strong and it was a well-established Sydney bookshop. It was run by the Theosophical Society. If you were interested in exploring different avenues and aspects of spirituality, issues and perspectives that you were unfamiliar with, this was the place to go. I was a regular peruser and an occasional purchaser.

Why did I buy the book? I was at that stage of life when I wanted to know everything about everything. I felt I should have a psychological perspective on how people are 'made', and in particular, what governs the dynamics of relationships between people. I wasn't just thinking about families, although of course, Virginia Satir says this is the place to begin. I think I also thought that I would be a parent at some point, and it was important to have some idea about parenting.

Curiously, one of the comments on the back cover mentioned bibliotherapy, a word that I had never heard of, or thought about again until quite recently, when I purchased *Reading the Seasons* by Germaine Leece and Sonya Tsakalakis.

Virginia Satir worked in family therapy in California. She talks about troubled families and nurturing families. It was a difficult dichotomy for me. I would not have described the family I grew up in as troubled, but I would have squirmed rather than describe it as nurturing. I would have described it in terms of having rules about fairness and decency, honesty and excellence, but I would have veered away from terms that suggested strong positive feelings of each person for the others. The framework for living seemed to come from the outside, not the inside.

That may seem like an odd comment, but outside and inside is a helpful dichotomy. Society's rules are rules that come from the outside. Religious rules come from the outside; God is something external, and the rules come from there. Even personal life in religion comes from the outside: forgiveness, love, humility, all come from the outside, from Jesus, the church. The inside is merely he/she who submits.

If that is the context, then people-making is challenging, because she starts with the concept of self-worth, only it is not a concept, it is a feeling. She describes it as a pot, like a cauldron, and the question is: how full or empty is the pot? Which is to say, how good do you feel about yourself? She says the importance of the pot is that it is the place from which you can do things. It is your resource and your resilience. With a strong sense of self-worth, one can even survive defeats and failures.

There are three other concepts in Satir's framework: communication (how people make meaning with one another), rules that govern feeling and acting (which creates a system), and how people relate beyond the family (links to groups, organisations and society). Troubled families are characterised by low feelings of self-worth, communication that is not clear – it is indirect, vague and not really honest, rules that are rigid and absolute, and links to society that are fearful, placating and blaming.

When Satir is discussing the rules that families devise, she says the rules often tend to block family members from feeling empathy with each other. Each person lives in a separate world, which is not necessarily bad, but they are unable to share their worlds with each other. The feeling is "if I shared that, I would be demolished": perhaps with scorn, or expressions of superiority, or unwillingness to listen.

Satir observes that people in troubled families may recognise the dysfunctionality, but they don't know what to do about it, and the chances of getting everybody to work on improving things are scant.

She quotes from *The Prophet* by Kahlil Gibran: "Let there be spaces in your togetherness". But it is one thing to have an ideal about parents as admirable couples, and another to start to take the small steps that might move you in that direction, in whatever position one finds oneself in the family configuration.

In my early twenties, my feeling was that I had survived the family. I had grown up, probably deficient in every one of the four aspects Satir discussed, and if I had a family of my own, it didn't have to reflect the less satisfactory aspects of the family I had grown up in. I wasn't casting blame, and I accepted my own part in the dynamics of the family, such as I understood it. The central issue was how to move from an articulated ideal towards changing reality. Could I change reality?

Since then, there have been broken relationships, in which children have been involved. One can agonise about the past, and joust with blame, either pointing the dagger at someone else or at oneself. Is there a way beyond that morass, responsibly?

Rather than having an answer, I have a story. It's from a song called "Clark Gable" by The Postal Service. It struck the writer, one day on the train, that he had been waiting all his life for a love that would look and sound like a movie. Accordingly, he rented a camera and called an ex-girlfriend. He said to her: "I need you to pretend that we are in love again." With the camera set up, he kisses her "in a style Clark Gable would have admired. I thought it classic!"

He ends with saying, "Do you ever get the fear that your perfect verse is just a lie you tell yourself to get by?" (The songwriters were Benjamin Gibbard and Jimmy Tamborello.)

Life is unscripted and we are imperfect. I think the two writers tell the story beautifully, and not out of despair. Perhaps the seeds of wisdom look like this story.

Why has this book surfaced again? Have Virginia Satir's insights become part of our society's received truths? Are they part of my own repertoire of rules and values? Satir was writing at a time of great changes in families, and in the lives of men and women, perhaps particularly women. At the end of her book she says, "If the next fifty years just equal the changes of the last fifty years, then by the year 2020, the family could look quite different" (pp. 302-303).

She thought we were heading towards "a more responsible human who can make choices; who can plan according to his needs, and not according to someone else's plans for him; someone who will recognise that there are differences concerning people as well as predictable similarities" (p. 303). She sees the coming end of relationships based on force, obedience and stereotypes.

However, life is also fickle and intransigent. It has been fifty years (it is now 2023), and it is still easier to see the faults rather than the sweetness of family life, or more generally, relationships between people. In a general, ideological sense, one is tempted to say relationships are less reliant on force, obedience and stereotypes. Those values are not nearly so dominant in society as they were in 1972. Yet, these values are still evident in society, and are still widely considered to be justified.

And, one of the problems of self-esteem is what happens when it is appropriated as the core value. This informs the title of a book published in 2008: *The Self-Esteem Trap*, by Polly Young-Eisendrath. The book has a long sub-title: "Raising confident and compassionate kids in an age of self-importance". I found the book at a book fair a couple of years ago. As is sometimes the case at book fairs, the book was augmented with an inscribed greeting complimenting the book: "Dear Adam and Georgie-girl, This is without doubt the best book I've ever read about child-raising. It gives deep PRINCIPLES upon which to base our decisions, rather than 'rules' which I hate. It would have liberated me to have clear boundaries because they have meaning and deep purpose, rather than simply to win."

The central theme of the book is parents who think that their children are 'special', and that this is the foundation of self-esteem.

The author shows how this mantra leads to unbalanced, stressed children rather than balanced children who know how to be successful in the world. It is interesting how the agenda for useful talk about parenting has changed over fifty years, although I would say the themes are similar.

Satir talks about rules in troubled families being rigid and arbitrary, while Young-Eisendrath talks about the need for principles that are understood rather than rules that are merely applied and enforced. There is a commonality here.

The recent book talks about children being given scope to face adversity rather than being artificially protected. This suggests parenting that is much more intrusive than in 1972; in this respect the themes have shifted.

Some of the language is more developed in the recent book. There is talk about emotional maturity, a subject that was barely evident in the 1970s. I can see how the new book is a development from the themes that Virginia Satir addressed. I suppose that a concept has to be around before you can take it and build upon it. My one disappointment about the new book is that Satir does not get a mention in the bibliography.

It's strange, isn't it, how a book can be pivotal in social change in one generation, and then a generation later, another well-known, active commentator can seem not to be aware of her forebear? I am sure the two women would have been good comrades.

Why has this book surfaced again? I haven't really answered the question, although the surfacing of Polly Young-Eisendrath's book recently suggests that the themes of family functioning and child-raising remain pertinent. And as Confucius said, if families functioned well, the whole world would be in harmony.

## 21. The Consolations of Philosophy and The Pleasures and Sorrows of Work

By Alain de Botton, the former published in 2000, and the latter published in 2009.

I don't have a photographic memory, so I don't remember all the books I have in my library. This is particularly true if I haven't spent much time with the book. Many books I have acquired with the thought that they look interesting, and I will probably get to read them one day. I knew I had a book by Alain de Botton, but I couldn't remember which one it was. I thought it was either *The Consolations of Philosophy* or *The Pleasures and Sorrows of Work*.

I knew I had bought the book because de Botton seemed like an interesting person who wrote about a wide range of issues that are of interest to ordinary people. I didn't know what particular perspective he held, but he was a writer who had achieved popularity around the world.

I didn't buy *The Consolations of Philosophy* at the book fair because I guessed, wrongly, that it was the book I had. I would call this atypical behaviour. Usually, I would have bought the book. Anyway, it was no loss, because I got to spend some time with the other book, *The Pleasures and Sorrows of Work*. And I managed to find *Consolations of Philosophy* in an online second-hand bookstore and ordered it.

However, things do not always go according to plan. I got an email to say the book had been delivered. I didn't think this was the case, and when I went out to the driveway to see, the book was not there. As proof of delivery, the email contained a photo taken by the courier of the delivery spot, a letterbox. It was not my letterbox.

There is a house about half a kilometre away from me which has a similar address, so it was no surprise to me that the photo was of the letterbox at that house. I sent an email back to the company saying that the parcel was not delivered to my address, but to somewhere else. Their response was to send me the photo again, as if to say: "See! We really have delivered the parcel." They included the text of their policy about leaving the parcel in a "safe place" if the person is not at home.

I replied to say that this was not my letterbox, and the inclusion of the text of the policy was not relevant if the safe place was not at my address. Later, someone rang me and I had to explain that the parcel was obviously dropped at the house which has a similar, but different, address to me. I said that I wanted the courier to retrieve the parcel and deliver it to me, at the correct address.

The person undertook to fulfil my request, although I didn't hear any apology. I got the feeling that they were disappointed that the photo, which was their incontrovertible proof of delivery, had not satisfied me. Two days later, I have yet to see *Consolations of Philosophy*. I am sure there is a joke in this.

**Addendum:** Later the same day: the parcel arrived! The parcel contained two books, so the postman had to squeeze it in, but he managed to fit it into my letterbox. It took me just as much time to jiggle it out of the letterbox. Amusingly, the two books were both Penguin Classics. In the later section, "About Personal Libraries", of which I have already written a draft, there is a discussion of the physical appearance of Penguin Classics. For the record, my copy of *The Consolations of Philosophy* has an orange and white cover, with the text in black. The edition dates from 2008. The other book was *The Road Less Travelled*, by M. Scott Peck, and it would fit well among books that were pink and red. It dates from 2020.

In the meantime, I have read Wikipedia's article on de Botton, and indeed he is an interesting man. As a young man he was all set to follow the academic pathway, but he was diverted, or distracted, into writing books. I can relate to that. I think there is far more scope to write something satisfying in a book than there is in producing an academic thesis. The same strictures do not apply. And yet, it is easy to have opinions. I have written elsewhere that one definition of humans is that they are a repository of opinions.

The Wikipedia article on de Botton observes that a negative review of *The Pleasures and Sorrows of Work* was published in the *New York Times*. I puzzled about this. I have studied the book; I have not yet read it all, but I am familiar with it and what it is seeking to do. The Wikipedia writer described the book as "a survey of ten different jobs, including accountancy, rocket science and biscuit manufacture. The book, a piece of narrative non-fiction, includes two hundred original images and aims to unlock the beauty, interest and occasional horror of the modern world of work." I think this describes the book well enough. I would describe it as a meditative piece on the subjective experience of various types of work. It contrasts this with the practical need to earn money, so it highlights the tension between these two perspectives.

So, I wondered, what would a negative review consist of? I can imagine a person not being interested in the book, but if that is the case, my advice would be not to read the book. When you pick the book up, you can quickly see that it is not a thesis on work; it is not a sociological study. It does not analyse; it observes from the worker's perspective. I was prompted to try and find the review and some discussion about it.

And yes, I did find a discussion of the review. One person said of the book, "It's a shame the book isn't better, because discussion is needed about the nature of work." To which my response would have been: "That's not the book I wrote, and I didn't claim to have written that book!" It's funny when people tell other people what book they should have written.

Another respondent referred to "the almost inescapable pomposity of the project" but admitted that he/she hadn't read the book, which itself suggests the almost inescapable pomposity of the respondent. The review, by Caleb Crain, was quite vicious, not simply critical. Another respondent suggested that Crain merely thought differently to de Botton, so he didn't like the book. This seems to underplay the vitriol contained in the review.

De Botton apparently responded to the review with his own, apparently uncharacteristic, vitriol. In part, he said "It is a review driven by an almost manic desire to bad-mouth and perversely depreciate anything of value. The accusations you level at me are simply extraordinary. I genuinely hope that you will find yourself on the receiving end of such a daft review some time very soon – so that you can grow up and start to take some responsibility for your work as a reviewer." There was more, but I won't repeat it.

Another respondent came in at this point and said, "Mr. Crain, I'm afraid your review only seems to indicate that you missed the point of Alain de Botton's latest work — and indeed, that you miss the point of a great deal of his work. Certainly, de Botton is a bit more of a documentarian in *The Pleasures and Sorrows of Work* than you might usually find him in his more philosophical pieces, but the objective remains the same: getting the reader to think in a different way about a subject that might not be given enough thought. De Botton painted some incredibly human characters that were quite poignant in many ways, though your selected quotes taken out of context indeed give them a mocking tone that the book itself lacked. A dry sense of humor about certain things is not the same thing as contempt."

This discussion went on for some time. I choose to end it with the following comment, by another correspondent: "Welcome to the American publishing business, Alain. I should say I'm currently reading Pleasure/Sorrow and it's a cracking read, certainly puts one into a tangential state of mind without bleating about how and what I should think about the state of the modern world."

Yes, I do think that de Botton painted pictures of people at work that were poignant, as the respondent above observed. However, I return to the expression I used above: it is a meditative study of people at work. It is not a rationalist deconstruction of work as a context.

From that standpoint, anything that evokes emotional responses becomes 'pompous'. It is a combative position. Perhaps that is why the review drew such a pained response from de Botton.

I prefer not to say that the pictures de Botton painted were poignant. Certainly the people described did not see themselves as objects of sympathy. But if they evoked sympathy in the reader, that seems like an avenue towards a deeper understanding of the exigencies of work, which, I think, was de Botton's purpose in producing the book. (The thesaurus bundles 'exigency' with words like antagonism, difficulty, toughness, trial, perverseness, intricacy, and knot. Work can be all of that.)

One of the 'jobs' that de Botton observed was painting. I was drawn to that because my father was a painter. But we differ, because my father was a painter of houses, and de Botton's painter was a painter of trees, an artistic painter. Although, I remember my father mixing and matching colours, and I remember watching him paint, and observing the care that he took. But, you might say, that is the care of a craftsman, not the inspiration of an artist.

I think that art and craft are yin and yang. Together they achieve balance and wholeness.

The painter de Botton examines is Stephen Taylor, a resident of Colchester. That was of interest to me because one of my great great grandfathers was born there (in October 1829). He ended up in London and became a child pickpocket, and was sent to Australia as a convict in 1846. Stephen Taylor is not a model of outstanding success, fortune and fame, but then, here he is in de Botton's book. De Botton spends the chapter watching Taylor as he goes about his daily business, which at this point is painting the same tree every day for three years, an oak tree which is 250 years old.

"His devoted look at a tree is an attempt to push the self aside and recognise all that is other and beyond us" (p. 181). To me, these are bold words. De Botton is presuming the perspective of the artist.

Either he is being pompous, a judgement to which the critic leapt so readily, or he is attempting something awesome: to speak for the painter who only speaks through the canvas. I believe there was mutual respect between them. Taylor refers to *The Pleasures and Sorrows of Work* on his website (yes, he has a website).

The other passage which I liked was this: "Taylor knows that he is creating things which exceed him. He has a chance to get himself right on the canvas in a way that he cannot in the run of his ordinary life" (p. 182). Perhaps that is true of all art, and writing, and crafts, and even all the products of work, whatever that work is – if it is done with devotion and integrity.

Taylor and de Botton must have discussed concepts of what art is, because de Botton offers the philosopher Hegel's view of art as Taylor's view. Hegel defined art (and music) as the "sensuous presentation of ideas". We need it because many important truths will not impress themselves on our consciousness unless they have been moulded from sensory, emotive material. It may only be when we are standing in front of a painting of an oak tree that we understand the significance of nature, as opposed to accepting that as a precept.

There was an exhibition of the pictures of the oak tree, and some of the pictures sold. Taken as a whole, Taylor's project is less remunerative than if he had been working as a plumber. And yet, Taylor's mind is already set on the next project, which will be about painting water in a river.

What is my project? To write the story. What is it the story of? The water that flows past me in the river.

Having obtained the book, *The Consolations of Philosophy*, I need to say something about it. If the title of the book sounds like a pre-existing statement, it is. It is drawn from a book of that name by Boethius, a Roman senator who was put to death in 524 AD, and who pondered philosophy while he was imprisoned, penning the book.

The connotations of the word 'philosopher' have changed over the years. I engage in activities that could be considered philosophy, but I have always been wary of that tag.

When you link philosophy with consolations, it is even worse. It then sounds like an activity you would gainfully engage in only if you were imprisoned. Otherwise, wouldn't you be working, or gardening, or conducting business affairs? Or travelling or having a family? Philosophy has the whiff of the armchair about it, the pipe and the disdain for ordinary life, an aloofness.

Perhaps the environment de Botton was brought up in did not lead him to this connotation. He had what I would call a classical education. And we are, after all, talking about connotations, not anything more substantial than that. But it is a widespread view that philosophy is irrelevant, a bunch of ideas with no apparent application to everyday life. It is just for people who like to argue. Mark Knopfler of Dire Straits said it in his song, "Industrial Disease": "Philosophy is useless, theology is worse".

So, I have expressed my reservations. What does the book have to say?

It would be fair to say the book is a primer for philosophy, done in a certain way. He takes six philosophers and six topics of human concern, and uses each of the philosophers to offer a perspective on each of the topics. Thus, Socrates gives an introduction to popularity versus sound thinking, Epicurus provides a perspective on the relationship between desires and happiness, Seneca addresses frustration, Montaigne offers insight into dealing with inadequacy, Schopenhauer gives a philosophical view of having a broken heart, and Nietzsche confronts difficulties.

In so doing, he offends some people, who think that philosophy should not be linked with self-help. However, I think there are just as many people who think that if you can't find some application in ordinary life of the philosophy that you choose to read, you are being perverse and elitist.

What comes through *The Consolations of Philosophy* is a championing of the idea of the rational mind. In discussing Seneca, he talks about anger. Sometimes people respond to a frustrating situation with an outburst (somewhat like de Botton did in response to the disparaging review of *The Pleasures and Sorrows of Work*). What usually happens is that the person apologises later, and says they were overcome by an emotion, implying that they had no control over it.

Seneca says (as de Botton explains) that outbursts are the result of rationally held ideas, not uncontrollable emotions. They arise because the person has dangerously optimistic ideas about the nature of the world. The truth is, our expectations are not justifiable. We felt entitled to something, and that was not the nature of the reality. By changing our ideas, we can avoid anger.

I think there is some truth in this, but one can go in several different directions from this point. Seneca's, and de Botton's, are not the only way to think about it. My feeling is that de Botton's reasoning is predicated on certainty. He begins in certainty, and through his perception and reasoning, he moves towards certainty. There are other approaches. One of them is indicated by indigenous people, as we shall see.

Nevertheless, Ancient Greek philosophy has influenced thinking in the west for two thousand years. Seneca said: "We may be powerless to alter certain events, but we remain free to choose our attitude towards them." This sentiment, which in trivial circumstances may seem trite, was the essence of Viktor Frankl's book, *Man's Search for Meaning*, which he wrote in 1946 after coming out of Auschwitz: "It did not really matter what we expected from life, but rather, what life expected from us. We needed to stop asking about the meaning of life, and instead to think of ourselves as those who were being questioned by life – daily and hourly" (p. 98).

However, there is rather more in what Frankl said than merely changing his ideas, an exercise in reasoning. It is a statement that calls upon what is deep in us. There is a mother in Oriah Mountain Dreamer's book, *The Invitation*, another book that I found. The mother is exhausted, but she gets up in the morning because her child needs to be fed. It is a deep thing to find that strength. It is not merely reasoning; that is not enough.

## 22. Books on Indigenous People and Indigenous Knowledge

The book I wrote called *Future* addressed the flood of ideas about where humanity is going and what it will take for us to have a viable future on this planet. I have a feeling I will come back to that book, to extend it, perhaps to amend it, although I think it contains valuable themes for us to contemplate. I apologise for saying 'us'. It's an easy temptation to bundle us all together as if we were the same. In critical ways we are the same: the collectivity of our behaviour brings us into a largely common fate. But in many contexts it is just not helpful to bundle 'us' in this way. We need to make distinctions between the different types of behaviour that different humans, and human groups, engage in.

One of the themes I took on in that book was indigenous peoples and indigenous knowledge. There are commonalities between indigenous people around the world, a fact of enormous significance, but it is fair to say that the indigenous people of Australia are special, because their habitation of this continent goes back so far it dwarfs comparison with people anywhere else in the world. In my book I examined evidence of previous civilisations on earth, and currently the accepted view is that the earliest societies go back to around 9,000 BCE. By contrast, the Aborigines have been on the Australian continent for probably more than 60,000 years, continuously and without ever having been invaded.

We know the sins of civilisation: the exploitation of natural resources until they are exhausted, the ignoring of the effects of human activity on the global climate, the perpetuation of iniquitous hierarchies and unbalanced distribution of wealth, the continuation of wars and quests for conquest of other societies. More simply, urban societies tend to create separation between people and alienation from the experience of nature.

In the book, I said that the challenge of indigenous people was that they still experienced the world in personal terms: "My country knows me", rather than taking the objective perspective where the natural world is merely seen as a potential resource for our lifestyle. Moreover, this shift is seen as necessary and inevitable. 'We' may have sympathy for the Aborigines, but their way is past, finished, defeated by the tide of civilisation. Why would we look back there? It sounds sentimental.

In the book, I called for humility in outlook and modesty in lifestyle. I admit, it seems rather too modest a proposal when bold moves seem to be called for if we are to "fix the planet". At the same time, I asked that we/you seek "an immediate apprehension of life that sees it all as alive and sacred, and you as part of it" (p. 51). It was not even a proposal, because there was no plan attached to it. It was an appeal to change one's personal outlook.

I would accept it if someone said that this is actually radical ('radical' meaning "to get to the root of").

Since the First Fleet came to Botany Bay in 1788, there has been a prevailing view that the British brought civilisation, they opened up the country, and they improved it. The recent and current generations have been gracious enough to extend the gratitude for this to the (mostly) refugees who came to Australia after World War Two, even though many of them were not British. There were Greeks, Italians and eastern Europeans.

It is still a long stretch to bring Aboriginal people back into the conversation. Simply witness the fate of the Referendum in October 2023. A majority of people around the nation could not bring themselves to say 'Yes' to what was, essentially, a simple proposition: to recognise that Aboriginal people had lived on this continent for the longest time before the white people arrived. It is still soon after that referendum when I write, and some people may argue that the question was not so simple, and that not enough 'detail' was provided, but the fact remains that people could not bring themselves to say 'yes' to a proposition recognising and acknowledging the existence of Aboriginal people on this continent before them.

I spent some time at a pre-polling booth near my home, and one afternoon a young girl came up to me. She was ten to twelve years old. Straight away she asked me a serious question, without prelude: "Why would anybody vote 'No'?" I was quite taken aback, and knew instantly that I had to answer her with the same seriousness she had gifted me. I said, "I think that the people who plan to vote 'No' have a fear that if everyone votes 'Yes', then something awful will happen, like, the sky will fall in.

"I can assure you", I continued, "that if everyone votes 'Yes', the sky will not fall in. It is a simple matter of people recognising and acknowledging that the Aboriginal people were on this continent first, and for an inconceivably long time, and they deserve our respect."

If you were harsh, you might think I was being flippant. I was not, not in the least. Then I asked the girl, "Does this help in any way?"

She said, "Yes, actually, it helps a lot. Thank you." And off she went.

My answer is still the same. This morning I was looking at another book I had acquired recently at a book fair: *The Bond of Poetry*. This was quite unrelated to the topic of Aborigines in Australia. I am curious about a lot of things, and I enjoy a lot of different things. This book was of interest because it was published in 1939, in Melbourne, and it was intended for school-children. It was still necessary, in 1939, to argue for the fact that Australian poems were included. J.J. Stable, the editor, argues that the life experience of Australians (and Australian children) is not the same as that of people in Britain. Accordingly, poems that might mean a lot to British children meant very little to Australian children.

Stable goes on to argue that all the great poems are British, so Australian children still need to read them, but Australian poems should be included in the anthology. Accordingly, he includes "The Man from Snowy River" by Banjo Paterson, and "My Country" by Dorothea McKellar. But then, with great irony, he places the following epigraph on the title page: "Coelum non animum mutant qui trans mare current."

Of course, I did not know what it said, given my deficient education that did not include Latin. But I was curious enough to look it up. It said, "They change their sky, not their soul, who rush across the sea." It was from the Odes of Horace. My view is just that: people came to Australia with a given set of experiences, beliefs and perspectives, and even the people who did not have a mission to replicate it all in the new land (the leaders, the churches, the business people, the literate) brought it all anyway. It takes a long time – generations – to give up the old layers and really live in the new place.

Mr Stable was trying, in 1939, to take small steps towards an Australian perspective. Perhaps today he would have understood that part of the process of "becoming Australian" is to acknowledge the people who were there before you.

Perhaps it was not surprising that three books dealing with Aboriginal perspectives should turn up at the book fair. The books were:

- *Dark Emu*, by Bruce Pascoe
- *Talking to My Country*, by Stan Grant
- *Sand Talk*, by Tyson Yunkaporta.

I will look at them in date order.

## 23. Dark Emu

By Bruce Pascoe, published 2014.

*Dark Emu* won the Book of the Year Award in New South Wales in 2016, as well as the Indigenous Writer's Prize. It has been widely praised. Marcia Langton calls it "A profound challenge to conventional thinking about Aboriginal life on this continent." I was attracted to the book initially because of the title. A short time before this I had read a short booklet which explained the concept of Dark Emu. It referred to a shape that the Aborigines saw in the sky.

So far, this sounds similar to the patterns of stars that observers around the world in different ages have seen and named. The early astrologers/astronomers named constellations of stars for the shapes formed by the points of light made by the stars: Aries, Capricorn, Gemini, Libra and so on. But Dark Emu refers to a shape in the sky made by darkness, space where there are no visible stars. I had never had this concept; to me it was revolutionary. If this was common knowledge for other people, I had missed it! The booklet explained how Dark Emu, the shape in the sky, was helpful to Aborigines when moving from place to place. It connected with stories about the location and the history of places.

However, Bruce Pascoe's book was not about astronomy. It simply used the story of the Dark Emu. Baiame, the creator spirit, an emu, left the earth after its creation to reside as a dark shape in the Milky Way. The emu is linked with the grasslands of Australia, because the grasslands are where emus live. The book is about how Aboriginal people have lived on this continent.

Pascoe examined the writings of early explorers to see what they had to say about how the Aborigines lived. He compared this with other knowledge about Aborigines' ways of living. I grew up in the 1950s and 1960s, and the picture was simple: Aborigines were hunters and gatherers, and they were nomadic. Even in 1988, when I wrote my first book, *Places in the Bush*, a history of the Kyogle Shire in northern New South Wales, the picture was basically the same. The

Aborigines were said to live primarily on meat, such as wallabies and fish. There was not much mention of grains, vegetables or fruit.

I did wonder about that, but I had been asked to write the book in a hurry – less than twelve months – and I had no time to pursue particular topics in depth. I wonder what I would find if I were exploring the question now.

Pascoe's book presents ample evidence of Aboriginal agricultural endeavours, including farming grains and vegetables, harvesting, and storage of food. He shows evidence of groups of Aborigines living in substantial buildings, and in groups of buildings that one would have to say were villages. He describes sophisticated systems constructed for harvesting fish, and the use of wells in districts where water was scarcer. The picture he paints is of large-scale and well-established systems for managing food production, not of an impoverished people living tenuously and precariously.

In my book on Kyogle I wrote, "Early settlers commented on the general good health and fine physique of the Aborigines. 'Physically they were muscular, sinewy and of athletic build' (R.L. Dawson, *Australian Aboriginal Words and Names*, 1935). 'A great many of the young men were splendid physical types, very muscular and athletic' (W. Flick, *A Dying Race*, 1934)." (*Places in the Bush*, 1988, p. 8)

Kyogle was not a place where massacres occurred, and most of the early squatters had friendly relations with the local Aborigines. But you would have to say that relations were tinged with fears, because the Aborigines did not want the white people on their land, but the white people had superior weapons and numbers.

The Bundock family had Wyangerie Station, about ten kilometres to the north of Kyogle, from about 1840 until around 1900. They predated the dairy farming that took over the district from the 1880s. Mary Bundock was only a baby when her family moved there, and she spent most of her life on the station. She was close friends with the Aborigines, and was a keen observer of their ways. She took extensive notes, and in adult life became friends with an anthropologist at Sydney University.

She would ask the Aboriginal women if they would make her a piece to send to the university, and generally they would do so happily. As time went on, the Aborigines began to lose their skills. In one instance, she asked one of the young women if she would make a water vessel out of the leaf stalk of a Bangalow Palm, and the woman said, "Never I been make 'em; always tin can."

I know there are different ways of reading this story. It can be seen in terms of colonial condescension, but I think there was a warm human quality in the relationship, on both sides. More generally, it was always an impossible situation. I wrote, "For both sides the stakes were high. For the Aborigines the coming of the whites meant the invasion of their territory, the violation of their sacred places, and the annihilation of their hunting grounds and food sources. For the whites it was the securing of landholdings as a basis for prosperity in the new colony, and the pride of establishing themselves as successful pioneers at the frontiers of the empire" (p. 27).

Overshadowing the story of the Aborigines in Kyogle was the myth that held sway all through the 1800s and into the 1900s. I don't mean 'myth' as a false story; I mean it as an influential belief, that was held by white people and Aborigines alike. One version of this story was told by an old Aborigine known as Pom Pom. The story is located north of Kyogle, up in the mountains around Woodenbong. It was published in *The Queenslander* in the 1880s.

Pom Pom remembered life before the white man came. He said, in this time, a white man came and he climbed the mountain Jalgumbun. When he reached the top he met an Aboriginal man, and the two fought. In the battle, both men plunged over the cliff, locked together in their struggle. Thereafter, the Aborigines avoided the place, but the figure of the Aboriginal man could still be seen in the shadows made by the afternoon sun on the mountain. It seemed to be a tale foretelling the eventual demise of the Aboriginal race (p. 8).

There was another story that I heard from numerous people (this was in the 1980s). It concerned red cedars. Red cedar trees have beautiful wood, and it's nice to work, and it is not subject to rot. Accordingly, it was much sought after. But it is not found in many places. There were a few stands in some gullies on the far north coast of New South Wales, and a few at Barrington Tops in the vicinity of Newcastle. When it was discovered, there was a mad rush to cut it down and make some good money.

The rush did not even last long. Soon, the stands of red cedar were mostly gone. Nowadays it is still rare. I had one tree on my property at Horseshoe Creek near Kyogle, high up in a gully. It was still young. I left it there, and I didn't talk about it.

So, a story arose that the fate of the red cedar and the fate of the Aborigine were in parallel, although the tie was often expressed even more strongly, in terms of causality: "When the last red cedar tree falls, the last Aborigine will die." There was sad romance in it. It was, of course, simplistic, with little understanding of how Aboriginal blood, and culture, carry on.

Stories like this made it easier to accept the travails of Aboriginal people, as if to say that the most that could be done was to smooth the pillow of their dying bed. Pascoe says the view that prevailed towards the Aborigines fitted with the colonialists' view of their historical inevitability, as an extension of the British Empire. It was convenient, and it displaced any feelings of discomfort about having displaced the Aboriginal people from their lands, or thinking about the real significance of that.

Pascoe says it goes towards explaining how the observations of the early explorers, such as Major Thomas Mitchell and Charles Sturt, were ignored, indeed, not even noticed. Their diaries contained quite extensive reports of Aboriginal management of their environment, the active farming of their food, and the creation of surplus food of great quantity. Yet, he says, all of this is glossed over and the view of them as primitive savages persists even now.

He asks that Australia acknowledge the Aboriginal history of the country as evidenced by its food production achievements, and recognise the social and philosophical underpinnings of the culture that enabled those achievements. This is not a threat to the economy. Moreover, it would be good for Australia as a whole to recognise that the drive of private enterprise depends upon unlimited population growth, and we have been unable to reconcile this with the protection of key resources such as air quality, fertile soils and clean water.

These seem like formidable goals. There are the facts of colonialism and dispossession. We can't go back. But Pascoe says we are still in the situation that Aboriginal achievements are denied: their agricultural and spiritual achievements. This denial "is the single greatest impediment to intercultural understanding and, perhaps, to Australian moral well-being and economic prosperity" (p. 229).

As his last words, Pascoe is offering up a bold challenge. What would a discussion of the moral well-being of a nation look like? Furthermore, is it linked to economic prosperity? One comparison is modern Germany. Since the horror of Adolf Hitler's Third Reich, Germans have had to ask themselves what kind of people they are, whether they are a force for good in the world or not. Perhaps that is a good comparison. If we accept that the purpose and the widely employed practices of the early settlers were morally compromised (to understate it), who are we now? Are we a force for good in the world, or do our efforts betray blindness and hypocrisy?

"Coelum non animum mutant qui trans mare current": "They change their sky, not their soul, who rush across the sea."

**About books**

The focus of interest in this work is the books that turned up at book fairs that were books I already owned. But at times these books summon up other books. Bruce Pascoe's work drew on Bill Gammage's work, *The Biggest Estate on Earth* (2011). When I told one of my daughters about the effect Pascoe's work had on my perceptions, she gave me Gammage's book and said I should read that as well.

The idea that Aboriginal management of the land was minimal, almost random, and isolated, is persuasively defeated by the breadth of Gammage's examination, so much so that he can refer to Australia as a single 'estate'. Pascoe applauded Gammage's book when it came out, and Pascoe's book argues a similar thesis in a way that makes it accessible to a wide readership.

## 24. Talking to My Country

Stan Grant, published 2016.

If there was one incident that prompted Stan Grant's book, it was the slur on Adam Goodes, AFL star, in May 2013. It was a match between the Sydney Swans and Collingwood in Melbourne, and someone in the crowd yelled out "Ape!" There are several ways you can look at this: it was a racial slur, and/or it was intended to knock him off his game, or, you can see it merely as part of the rough-house, hurly-burly atmosphere of a football match.

The point of a racial slur is to dig at the underlying beliefs a person may have as to their inherent inferiority. But even in places where such conduct is tolerated, people generally learn some finesse about what lines not to cross. It gets to be quite a sophisticated art: how to throw an insult (or a punch) that incites someone, but not to step over the line yourself, the line where punishment would be attracted to yourself. It is a subtle art of sensing where that line is in particular situations.

For his part, Adam Goodes could have been ignored the insult, and the moment probably would have passed without further comment. However, he chose to call it out. He pointed out the person, who happened to be a thirteen-year-old girl, and she was removed from the stadium. In the ensuing furore, the girl apologised, and said she had not realised how deeply it had affected him.

However, some commentators defended the right of spectators to boo players on the field, either in disapproval of their play or their behaviour. Of course, this could hardly include calling a player an ape. In the defence of 'rights', some things get overlooked. Grant, who has forged a friendship with Goodes, said Goodes was told to toughen up, to get over it. This is part of the game of delivering an insult then retreating behind the line. Some people were outraged at the mere suggestion that a racial insult had been used.

Grant maintains that Goodes was eventually driven out of the game in 2015, even after having been awarded Australian of the Year in 2014. Grant responds to the claim that we should leave our history behind us with the retort: "History is not past for us." He points to Marcia Langton's comment: "There is a primal, deep-seated racism here [in Australia]" that she had hoped we had moved beyond (p. 207).

What do I think? I think that, at a collective level, the most that can happen is what did happen: policies can be devised, public statements can be made, structures can be set up. The AFL Players' Association and all the captains released an open statement that included the words "We encourage supporters to demonstrate zero tolerance and report any behaviour which vilifies a person on the basis of their personal characteristics, such as race, religion, gender or sexual orientation."

However, from a combative mindset, all this means is that more and more restrictions are being placed on my behaviour. It can lead to angry, rhetorical claims: is this the kind of society we are heading towards?

I come back to the girl who shouted the insult. She obviously thought it was okay to shout out an insult in public. The usual defence is to say it was just a joke. So, she came from a family where insults were allowed, or perhaps it was that insults were allowed in the atmosphere of a football match. Personally, I have zero tolerance for 'jokes' that include insults of other persons. Not that I am perfect, but I am on guard against temptations to indulge in such behaviour. It takes you down a road where things can only get worse, and the triumphs, if there be any, are petty.

Adam Goodes had already won his prominence by his exceptional play and his success in football, so there were many people ready to support him. But in the atmosphere of crowd statements, it's hard to move past win and lose. It is not an advance if the people who want to insult or boo merely think that now they are being forced to be quiet and not to "have their fun". The realisation that is necessary is a personal one. It is that insulting people is not a positive thing, whatever characteristic is the target: Aboriginal, wog, stupid, carrot-head, girl.

This is the inherent weakness of anti-discrimination laws: they target an ever-growing list of specific characteristics, but not the more general principle. To take the employment context, the principle is that if you are employing a person for a job, you should only have regard to the qualities that are important for doing the job, the "inherent requirements of the job" to use the legal terminology. You should not use other characteristics to rule a person out, for example, their race, age, or sex.

You can't have laws stopping people from insulting each other, but that should show us that there needs to be a discussion about more than what laws to pass. A parent might say to their children, "Don't do that." In other social contexts there are softer and firmer ways of cultivating an environment where people do not insult each other. It would be a fundamental shift in the social atmosphere.

Stan Grant ends his book with the concept of home. His home is Australia, and home is a place where you should feel safe and welcome, a place where you belong. Today, many people call Australia home, but that concept of home needs to be broad and inclusive. At the least, it should consciously and deliberately include the people who were the First Australians.

If you think about the now-accepted practice of acknowledging Aboriginal people at the start of public events: the Acknowledgment of Country, and then consider the words of the National Anthem, and then the words of the Bruce Woodley song, "I Am Australian", the place where I think more emphasis is needed is on the land itself.

"Advance Australia Fair", I think, is fair enough as a national song. It was written by Scottish-born composer Peter Dodds McCormick in 1878, and it reflects the time when it was written, when the idea of Australia as one, unified nation was growing. The lyrics of Bruce Woodley's song, however, could be called 'mature'. It understands and accepts the whole of Australia's history: the Aboriginal stewardship of the land, the coming of white people in 1788 that was an invasion, the colonial period, and the milestones to our current times such as the two world wars.

More importantly, Woodley's song calls upon the singer to identify with the place that is Australia: "I am Australian"! And it includes everyone in that identification: "I am, you are, we are Australian". I find that very powerful. It has been sung with Aboriginal singers and people who come from many different nations, in chorus.

The problem for non-Aboriginal people, then, is that they are usurpers. There was never a moment when they were accepted by this place. No matter if you are third, fourth or fifth generation, there was never a point when you became Australian. A birth certificate or a certificate of naturalisation doesn't do it; they are merely records of external facts.

My experience was this. I was sitting in my backyard, and a kookaburra came to sit on the clothes line. My clothes line, its perch. It did not laugh. Instead, it looked at me, one eye sideways.

I said (not talking, just mind), "I been Australia long time: mother, father, long way back." Kookaburra, he no go, he still look me. (And now I am thinking in Aboriginal, like the earth, no sophisticated grammar, just the elements.) "I say (in mind), I grow roots down; this home now, nowhere else." There are tears in this.

Next morning, two kookaburras laughed in the gum tree next door. I think: "That welcome call. I stay now."

So, the land must accept us, whoever we are, if we respect it. In the secular mind, it is about respect. But actually, the land is sacred, and we are one with it. I think Bruce Pascoe is talking about a partnership between Aborigines and the land that only occurs when the people and the land are one. There is no conquering, no beating the land into submission. One accepts it, and learns how to work with it. This could be called taming, but even that might be too bold a word.

Or, it's like the Kalihari Bushmen who hear the stars talk, and it's part of existence. There are no walls between things. The *Tao Te Ching* talks about a mindset: "Can you coax your mind from its wandering and keep to the original oneness? Can you love people and lead them without imposing your will? Can you deal with the most vital matters by letting events take their course? Giving birth and nourishing, having without possessing, leading and trying not to control: this is the supreme virtue." (Verse 10)

It is only with this improbable Chinese text (by Lao Tsu, about 500 BCE) with its seemingly nonsensical observations that I can see a viable way of living that is not based on force that is afterwards justified as destiny.

## 25. Sand Talk

By Tyson Yunkaporta, published 2019.

It seems fitting that the next book to turn up at the book fair was Tyson Yunkaporta's book, *Sand Talk*. It is recent: 2019. It is fitting because it deals with the more intangible aspects of Aboriginal culture, namely, the way they think. Bruce Pascoe calls it "a book of cultural and philosophic intrigue".

I could relate Tyson's book to my time as a commentator on teaching and training. He was concerned with what knowledge indigenous people held. The simplistic outsider's concept is that there is nothing, because Aboriginal people mostly died out. By 'outsider', I mean people who do not belong to an Aboriginal group. It follows from what Pascoe and Grant talked about that this is a widespread perception: there is no longer any Aboriginal knowledge.

Tyson's addresses this early on: "Our knowledge endures because everybody carries a part of it, no matter how fragmentary" (p. 14). But he is not really addressing it, he is just making an observation as he goes. The book itself is sufficient answer.

I ask, what is the nature of this knowledge? And I think in terms of learning styles. Some people like to be involved actively and emotionally in order to learn. Some people like to reflect on what is being learned, so their thinking is about looking at a thing from different viewpoints. Some people operate more abstractly, and they think in terms of concepts, theories and processes rather than getting involved with emotions; they like structures and planning. Some people are focused from the beginning on pragmatics: how can I apply this? And they experiment with the tools available.

I learned as a teacher and trainer that I had to try to appeal to these different perspectives in order to engage people who had different learning styles. Now I want to understand how Tyson's knowledge compares with this. Tyson was saying that attempts to include the indigenous perspective were usually polite but formulaic, a carefully curated view through a window.

He says the indigenous perspective recognises patterns in things and connections between things. It is difficult in language because you can only say things like "time is non-linear" without offering much understanding of what this means. It is only possible to convey some of this through stories. Already one wonders if this will be unsatisfying.

Then, Tyson says one needs to begin with the question of who has the knowledge. Who carries it, and what of it is relevant to the problems of today? From there, one goes to statements about the knowledge being stored in the landscape: in rivers and hills, in rocks and twists in trails one can hardly see.

Tyson has devised a number of symbols to convey different aspects of the knowledge. One consists of the "greater than" and the "less than" symbols side by side. One meaning is that many problems in the world arise when one person or group sees itself as superior to others. They are narcissists; they might use the language of equality, but they break those very rules and break down harmonious society.

The signs also stand for types of meat, say, marsupials and birds, and the direction of the lines can be related to the legs of the animals. And in them can be seen the rules for marriages: the kinship system. Tyson goes on to talk about the rules for fighting, traditional fighting where the weapons were stone knives, and how these fights had to end: with the winner being cut up the same as the loser. It carries the subtext that it helps to try to see your opponent's point of view.

The "greater than thou" point of view reminds us of abuse hurled at football matches: "Ape!" Rather, the thing to strive for is to understand who you are on earth and where you have come from, and to carry this with integrity, and let it infuse everything you do. And Tyson is learning how to learn from everyone: he is not greater than, and not less than.

Another image Tyson uses is of several circles layered on top of each other. It looks like a rose to me. He says it represents the three dimensions of time: past, present and future, but they all exist at once. It all exists at once, and it is constantly moving, and we must move with it. Or, it is about generations of humans: we are child, adult, parent, grandparent, and have to be able to see from each of these perspectives. Or, you can relate it to contemporary views of physics, where it is no longer possible to be outside, an objective observer. Life is a thing of possibility. Schrodinger's cat may be dead or alive, at the same moment in time.

Knowledge is not about control and exploitation. It is a different perspective. It is the acceptance of subjectivity, of working with creation, rather than on it. What are the things that are sustainable? Subjectivity suggests family and community, interdependence. It does not fit with the "greater than/less than" paradigm.

Tyson paints modern society as a catastrophic system based on a flawed perspective on the basic laws of the earth, one that requires ever-increasing growth in deference to the economic myth of demand and supply. His assessment is blunt. But perhaps creation's systems keep going because people still have kinship, and threads of connection to land and nature and its rhythms. And because of contentment with that. It is a way of being and a pattern of logic.

Along the way, Tyson dispenses with the crude terms, 'black' and 'white'. That is a relief. Even the First Fleet was not wholly 'white'. Over the years, people came to Australia from many countries, particularly during the goldrushes. This is the jettisoning of an unrealistic dichotomy.

He also observes that there is a struggle going on between 'indigenous knowledge' and ways of living and being. Indigenous knowledge becomes just something else to brand and defend. He says that people must work together to discern the patterns of creation out of living within a specific landscape. I think of the thousands of people who have sung the Bruce Woodley song, "I am

Australian" and have then thought about what that experience means, and how it should be taken forward and performed again.

He asks us to listen to many voices and stories, because patterns emerge and authenticity can be gauged. He goes on to talk about patterns in complex environments. He has an image for it: three wriggly lines in parallel. Unless we take the time to observe the whole, and think about how things affect each other, we will not see these patterns. Importantly, we ought not do this from the perspective of wanting to exert external control over the whole system.

The concept of strange attractors in systems comes from this endeavour. An attractor is a set of states toward which a system tends to evolve, for a wide variety of starting conditions of the system. An example would be a marble rolled into a round bowl. Its path is not predictable, but we know that it will come to rest at the bottom of the bowl. It is a strange confluence of concepts between indigenous life and chaos theory. Tyson brings the character of the person into this conversation: it is necessary for the person in the situation to be acting with integrity.

Tyson notes that not all strange attractors are benevolent. One loud person can shout ignorant or hateful things, and other people will follow suit. Tyson says that it is usually narcissism that is at work here, and it creates harm.

I think there is a thinking aspect to seeing patterns in life, but there is likewise a moral aspect. It is not a foregone conclusion that people will "discern the patterns of creation out of living within a specific landscape", but there is always an obligation to deal with other people decently. I am aware that this language creates a distinction that is not in creation.

Tyson talks about other things: spirit, yarns, how to appropriate modern technology without losing your soul, self-protection, the optimal use of consciousness given the predominance of rationality and logic in the modern world. He talks about what happens to our minds when we, individually and collectively, foster kinship, stories, and dreaming, and open ourselves to the ancestors. You add this to the talk about patterns in life and you might start to think you are shifting your foundations.

Tyson is saying there can be a dialogue between western/modern ways of thinking and indigenous thinking. He is ever-aware that anything that he says could be rigidified and therefore defeat the purpose. He says there are no trademarks on this knowledge, and it belongs to everyone. The symbols provide a foundation for playing with ideas.

There is a positive slant to Tyson's book. He thinks there are lots of opportunities for problem-solving and innovation through dialogue, that would lead to sustainability. From the indigenous perspective, this is not about risk management or guarantees of safety. It is about learning interdependence (us and the earth), but there are still major difficulties with trying to find amenable common ground between Aboriginal and mainstream societies. But the land still speaks, and the continued viability of the land for humans and animals depends on humans being custodians of the earth, not conquerors for the sake of cash.

The last image that Tyson leaves us with is a hand. Like all of his images, it means many things. Apart from anything else, it means that I am involved, and not at arm's length: You, me, Aboriginal, non-Aboriginal, we must be in this together. And it is a shift from the paradigm where the human changes the planet for his/her benefit, to a perception where there is an effect on ourselves when we try to effect some change on the earth.

I have tried to interpret Tyson Yunkaporta's ideas helpfully. He has thrown ideas out, like broadcasting seed, and I believe I have caught some, hopefully in a meaningful way. I think there is a commonality, something in the blood, between indigenous thought as Tyson describes it, and Taoist thought. A French writer, Francois Jullien, says that the Chinese never constructed a world of ideal forms, archetypes or pure essences that are separate from reality. Rather, they see the whole of reality as a regulated and continuous process, one that stems from the interaction of all the factors at play, which are both opposed and complementary (yin and yang).

In this thinking, order does not come from a model that is conceived separately from 'reality' and can be applied to things. Order is contained within the course of reality; it is "the way". The sage therefore sets out to illuminate the progress of things by looking for their internal coherence and then acting in accordance with it. In this mind, knowledge is not separate from action (p. 15).

As Tyson would say, too much of this hurts my head. One has to dance in and out of concrete things and abstract things, to and fro.

## 26. Sagaland

By Richard Fidler and Kari Gislason, published 2017.

It was with a measure of guilt that I saw this book at the book fair. I had bought the book, at a bookshop, soon after it was published, because I was interested in Iceland, and I knew that Richard Fidler was on ABC radio. But I hadn't yet read the book. Although this is true of many books in my library, seeing the book was like a personal reminder.

Why would I be interested in Iceland? It's nowhere near Australia, and it's nowhere near the route from Britain to Australia, so my ancestors would never have sailed past it. It's a smallish island up near the Arctic Circle. The climate would not entice me: snow and ice and long winters. It's not a metropolis: its total population is less than 300,000 people and there is really only one city.

However, Iceland crops up in the most unexpected ways. On Youtube, through the American radio station KEXP in Seattle, there was a young female singer, Soley Steffansdottir (spelled without the accents on the letters). Strange, lovely, and just on the edge of disturbing. Sometimes she uses a piano that sounds like the piano you might find in a house that hasn't been visited in decades, slightly off-key and wildly evocative.

She sings, "Have I danced with the devil?" and about sailing to an island where she tries to save a man from a burning house, but the doctors said he had never been there; he had gone to make war with himself. And about a rabbit that appears in her dream, and about singing wood to silence. How could you not take notice of that?

I study my family's history, and I always have to be resigned to the fact that the trails will run out at some point. The records will just not be there. I can't find a record for my great great grandmother's birth in Waterford, Ireland (her name is Sarah Crosby). I know it was in 1833 or 1831. But in Iceland, the records of families go back to around 870 AD, to right back when people first came to Iceland. They kept those records from the beginning. It takes a lot to understand the difference that makes to the way you see yourself, and the way you see the context of the family, and your relationship to them.

Sarah Crosby was torn from family twice over. She seems to have lost her family as a consequence of the potato famine in 1845-1850. But then she was in London and she was arrested. In desperation at being thrown out of a refuge, she had assaulted a policeman. And so, she was transported to Australia. I doubt she ever had any contact with family again, or even anyone from her childhood neighbourhood.

Iceland is so different. In Australia, there were people here going back well over 50,000 years. You might as well say, forever. Iceland was formed from the clash of tectonic plates twenty million years ago. It still has active volcanoes. Yet, no one lived there until around 880 AD. Some Vikings from Norway sailed there and settled, but there is also a story that prior to that, Irish monks sailed up from Ireland and settled. Not surprisingly, the Vikings displaced them when they arrived.

However, there are odd connections between Iceland and Australia. The very existence of the book is an instance. Richard Fidler and Kari Gislason, who was born in Reykjavik, met in Sydney, and happened to live near each other. After many conversations, they decided to go to Iceland and write a book about it together. The book is an odd mix of Richard's impressions, Kari's memories of his family, and the sagas that seem to be Iceland's gift to the world.

Another odd connection occurred when I was on a bush walk in Tasmania in 2019. There I was, with a group of people in the Tarkine area in the northwest, in the middle of dense, mountainous forest, and there was a plaque with a name on it: Jorgen Jorgensen. It quoted an extensive passage written by Jorgensen about the impenetrability of the forest we were standing in: "Fallen trees in every direction had interrupted our march, and it is a question whether any human beings, either civilised or savage, had ever visited this savage-looking country. Be that as it may, all about appeared well-calculated to arrest the progress of any traveller, sternly forbidding man to traverse those places which nature had selected for its own silent and awful repose."

Who was this man, when was this, and what was he doing here? He was Danish. At the age of fifteen he went to sea, and as a sailor he ended up at Port Jackson (Sydney) in 1800. From there he went to Van Diemen's Land (Tasmania), in fact, being part of the first settlements there in 1803. After that he went to England, where he had been before. It wasn't until 1825 that he came back to Australia, this time as a convict after he had been accused of, and sentenced for, theft.

Subsequently he led several expeditions to explore parts of Tasmania. It is from this period of time that the quote on the plaque derives. But in all of this adventuring, where does Iceland come in? In 1807 he was given command of a Danish vessel which was captured by the British, as Britain was then at war with Norway and Denmark. He was imprisoned in London.

He was given parole, and he sailed to Iceland with the intention of trading goods, but the governor of Iceland refused to allow him. Jorgensen then contrived to arrest the governor and proclaim himself the 'Protector' of Iceland. He held that position for two months until a Danish ship arrived and Jorgensen was taken back to England for punishment.

This whole story made sense to me because, accidently, I had recently read a book called *The English Dane* (by Sarah Bakewell, 2005). Thus, I had been immersed in the life story of this extraordinary adventurer, which included two months as the ruler of Iceland and a long connection to Tasmania. To complete the story, he ended up marrying a convict woman and he died in Tasmania.

When I learned that Iceland was renowned for stories that were called sagas, my thinking was flavoured by the memory of Jorgen Jorgensen's improbable adventures, of which I have only recounted a few. And I connected it to the history of the Vikings and their bold escapades that brought them to England as well as to many parts of Europe.

Gislason emphasised that a saga is not a story of gods and goddesses. It is a story of mortal men and women and their heroic and creative responses to the tribulations in their lives. It is a story of honour and valour rather than of magic. And it is a story that deals with the implications of family relationships. Gislason went back to Iceland from Australia to study sagas for his PhD, and discovered a family there that he had not met before.

The classic sagas come from the tenth century, in the days when the Vikings were dominant in Iceland. In the thirteenth century, many of the sagas were written down by a man called Snorri Sturluson. He is a national hero. He was a poet, politician and historian.

I have a volume called *Great Short Stories of the World*, published in 1964. I acquired it in my youth. Is Iceland represented? Indeed, it is. The book has a Scandinavian section, and the editors wanted to feature something from the Icelandic sagas, because they subsequently affected all the other Scandinavian countries. There are two tales from Iceland, along with two from Denmark, three from Norway, and three from Sweden. One of the two Icelandic tales is from Snorri Sturluson. (The other is anonymous, from the twelfth century.) The book says his work was founded upon oral tradition and the writings of earlier poets and historians.

The story in the book is "Baldr's Bale"; it is from the *Prose Edda*. The editors of the book say, "The saga literature of Iceland is very extensive. Over two hundred volumes of these narratives are still in existence" (p. 750). The *Prose Edda* is the best source we have for the Norse myths, which are the stories that seek to explain the creation of the world. We have co-opted their gods in naming our days of the week: Tyr, or Tiw, gives us Tuesday; Odin, also Woden, gives us Wednesday; Thor gives us Thursday; and Frigg gives us Friday.

Fidler says the challenge to Sturluson was to make the stories palatable to a Christian society, and he did this by nesting them inside a larger Christian universe. The main tribe of gods, the Aesir, are depicted as famous chieftains who have exceptional powers. When they die, their graves become sacred sites.

There is an interplay between humans, gods and animals, just as there is in Aboriginal stories. Gefjun, who was a daughter of the Aesir, used four giant oxen to plough up vast sweeps of land that would become her own, but the beasts were her own children. In similar manner, in Aboriginal lore, Baiame, the creator spirit, was an emu.

The first story that Fidler and Gislason tell is of a man named Audun (a name which is teasingly close to Odin). A thousand years ago, Audun was a poor farmhand who lived on the northwest coast of Iceland. He helped the captain of a ship that came to the harbour, and in return the captain took him on the ship to Greenland. There

Audun met a man who had captured a polar bear, and he bought the bear from him, using practically all the money he had.

Audun decided he would give the polar bear to the King of Denmark, who was said to be a good man. His journey went through Norway, and the King of Norway asked if he could purchase the bear. Audun declined, saying he had resolved to give it to the King of Denmark as a gift. Nevertheless, the King of Norway let him pass through.

In Denmark Audun ran out of money, and to obtain money he had to sell a half-share in the polar bear to one of the king's stewards. Despite this, the king welcomed him, accepted the bear and showered him with gifts. He even went to Rome. But eventually, he needed to go home to look after his mother. He went to see the King of Norway to tell him of his adventures, and the king was also generous to Audun.

Audun was acknowledged as a man of great good fortune, and many good people are descended from him. Fidler and Gislason remark that some of the characters in the story are real, that all the sagas are strange and therefore memorable, and that a connection to family descendants is made. Many living Icelanders can trace their ancestors all the way back to the saga characters.

*Sagaland* is a series of surprising and unexpected stories, swapping between the sagas and modern life. There is a chapter about Bobby Fischer, at one time the world chess champion. Chess has been prized in Iceland since long ago. In 1972, Reykjavik hosted a contest between Fischer and the reigning world champion, Russian Boris Spassky. The contest featured as much drama in Fischer's behaviour as in the contest itself. He was a genius but he was also a difficult person. Frequently, he would not even turn up for the games, and he made endless demands of the hosts. Yes, he did win the contest, in the best of twenty-four games, although it was not completely one-sided.

The mention of chess reminded me that I have a book on my shelves by another world chess champion, Garry Kasparov. Kasparov is notable because he was the first world chess champion to be beaten by a computer, in 1997. His book is called *Deep Thinking: Where Machine Intelligence Ends*. It was published in 2017 and I have owned it since about then. (Did I buy it at a book fair? I don't remember, but it has a bookmark in it from Berkelouw's Bookshop.) I tried to read it, but I just wasn't interested in thinking about machine intelligence at the time. And now, in 2023, artificial intelligence is really coming to the fore, with the emergence of tools like ChatGPT. I will probably have to revisit my resistance!

Much later in life, Fischer requested citizenship of Iceland. He was largely in disgrace in the USA, after a series of episodes of offensive behaviour that today might be understood as disintegrating mental health. He died in Iceland in 2008 and is buried there. Fidler and Gislason present this as yet another example of a strange life in the land of sagas. Late in life he went to see the Icelandic musician Bjork, and he was introduced to her. He said he loved soul music. She said, "Soul music is dead."

On Youtube, I discovered the Icelandic group Sigur Ros. After Pink Floyd and David Bowie, one thinks one has understood the concept of strangeness in music. However, metaphorically, Sigur Ros sounds like an isolated island in the North Atlantic Ocean, a long, long way from anywhere else. I would say that the singer sings falsetto, but I don't think I can. Falsetto is distinguished by counterpoint: the singer sings in an ordinary voice, and then at times sings in a much higher pitch. The Bee Gees explored the potential of this quirk in their later career (think, "Staying alive").

You can't say that about the singer in Sigur Ros because he never sings in a 'normal' voice. He sings permanently in the stratosphere. The instruments are those of a rock band, but some of their music is with an orchestra. I saw them (again, on Youtube) playing with the Disney Orchestra. The lyrics are just as odd. I read an interview with the band, and the singer said that some of their lyrics were Icelandic, some were English, some were in a hotch-potch language they had made up, and some of the words weren't words at all: they were just a flow of sounds that came to him.

Sigur Ros have been an active band for over twenty years. One of their clips on Youtube was eight hours long, and it consisted of music, much of it orchestral, some of it with that not-falsetto singing, played while the band was driving all the way around Iceland in a bus. Often, the footage was from a camera mounted on the front of the bus, driving through the Icelandic landscape. People must have known they were coming, because they would be waiting on the side of the road to give them sandwiches and drinks, and the bus would stop for a while.

Perhaps Sigur Ros sums up why I was slow in getting to *Sagaland*; I knew I would enjoy it, but I also knew I would have trouble connecting it to the rest of my experience. Yet there is something very evocative about it, like the title of one of Soley's albums: "Ask the Deep".

### 27. Modern Art and the Death of a Culture

By H.R. Rookmaaker, published, 1970.

The question that arises is: how did I choose the order of the books at Knox Grammar book fair? That would seem to make a difference, or it would seem to imply a point of view. Or, did I base the order on the order in which I found them? This is feasible, because I was organised for this visit, and I took photos of them on my phone.

Well, this is more or less true, bearing in mind that the books that seem to be grouped together were found in the same section at the book fair. But what also needs to be said is that I was somewhat overwhelmed by the number of books I found, and I thought it would be wasted energy to agonise over putting them in some other order.

I analysed it in terms of the years when the books were published. I even graphed it in an extremely old graph book I had in a stationery drawer in the library. But the graph didn't tell me anything. The years bounced around from recent to long past and back again. *Modern Art and the Death of a Culture* reminded me of this question of order, because it was definitely the oldest book I found that I owned, even older than *Peoplemaking*.

What attracted me to the book was the picture on the front cover: a man seated, a large and important man; but he was screaming and the top of his head was blown off, and there was the outline of a box in which he was contained. Moreover, it was as if the screams of the man could not be heard; it was an awful silence. It was both dreadful and intriguing. The painter was Francis Bacon; Rookmaaker names the painting as "Head VI". Otherwise, I have seen it called "Man and Beast". I learned that the painting was one of more than forty-five variants made by Bacon in the 1950s, and that it is a distortion of a highly respected portrait of Pope Innocent X made by the Spanish painter Diego Velazquez in the 1650s.

I had bought the book from the Scripture Book Centre in Sydney when it was fairly new (the sticker is in the book). I was in my early twenties and I think I was at Teacher's College because I needed to get qualified and get a job as soon as possible, and I only had a year to go in the course, but the study wasn't really fulfilling. And, I was still in church but I was feeling the urge to explore outside of the bounds of conservative Christianity. I, too, was still conservative, but I was looking at the fringes. Was Rookmaaker a good choice?

Probably, more to the point, there was something in that picture I identified with.

I was suspect about the title, although at that age I was attracted to bold expressions: "The death of a culture". What does that mean? Do cultures die? They change; they evolve; they may occasionally undergo radical transformations, but do they ever die? You could say it's a cheap, journalistic phrase. However, I wanted to explore everything, so I paid my money: two dollars sixty cents.

Secondly, was the obvious Christian perspective of the book going to be too much of a stricture, like the box enveloping the screaming man? I hoped not. I knew nothing about the history of art, so I was prepared to risk it.

The author maintains that art derives from the surrounding culture, and from its worldview, by which he means the Enlightenment and the Age of Reason. The profile of the author said that he was Dutch, and he had a doctorate in the history of art, but he had also explored the "*sub-cultures* (my emphasis) of pop and op, happenings and hippies, jazz and beat". Oh well, he could be interesting, I thought.

Nowadays, with experience, and coming from within the perspective fostered by the internet, I am suspicious of the idea of art representing a worldview. Perhaps this was true of the time when Rookmaaker wrote this book: people belonged to 'schools': Cubist, Modernist, Nihilist and so on, and they were promulgating a point of view. Francis Bacon was absorbed in the deconstruction of... what? A pope who was respected? The Catholic Church? Traditional portraits? Everything human?

Nowadays, there is such a variety of perspectives that the whole idea of schools starts to dissolve. Artists (I am thinking of musicians now) often do not have a reference group. They wouldn't classify themselves as jazz, pop, new age, rock, or country. And Dolly Parton has been inducted into the Rock and Roll Hall of Fame; so much for the country music arena. The reference points are fuzzier. It seems just too convenient for artists to fit into schools. But, we are in 1970.

Why was the pope's head blown off, causing him to scream? Why is he in a box? Rookmaaker says it is a caricature of mankind, "not humorous images but great cries of despair for lost values and lost greatness, for a humanity deprived of its freedom, love, rationality, everything that the great humanist painters had celebrated for centuries as they drew on their Christian and classical tradition" (p. 174). Okay, that's just what a conservative Christian is going to say. What does Bacon himself have to say?

Bacon explains his art in terms of humans' contemporary understanding of the world: "Man realises that he is an accident, that he is a completely futile being, that he has to play out the game without reason." He refers to Valezquez's painting of the pope, saying that people then were still "conditioned by certain types of religious possibilities, but these had now been cancelled out for him". Painting has become merely a game by which man distracts himself, and the challenge for the artist [of any type] is "to really deepen the game to be any good at all, so that he can make life a bit more exciting" (p. 174).

Rookmaaker goes on to talk about artists discovering the art in the ordinary, like Andy Warhol's painting of a Campbell's tomato soup can. But you can read that two ways; either it is a discovery of the art in the ordinary, and it is positive and happy, or it is an assertion that life is absurd and everything is cheap. Rookmaaker explores this from a philosophical perspective, and sees the result as the latter: the underpinning belief of our culture is that life is absurd and everything is cheap.

Rookmaaker follows the rise of the hippie movement of the late sixties, seeing it as a response to the coopting of art by the rich, the investment class, for whom the rationale for art was merely a pretentious façade. 'Happenings' were considered to be beyond the reach of pretentiousness because they were spontaneous. But there was an angry growl behind it all, typified by Allen Ginsberg's poem *Howl*: "I saw the best minds of my generation destroyed by madness, starving hysterical naked".

The pop art of this time, he says, was surrealistic, adopting some strange forms, but generally critical of the world. He quotes the artist Paul Klee, who said, in 1915, "The more horrible this world is, the more abstract art will be, while a happier world brings forth a more realistic art". But it led into an art progression that often blurred reality, the imagination, and the abstract. He concludes, "Art in a way is dying – as a high human endeavour. It has lost its romantic high quality, it is coming back to reality. We should not weep because another humanist myth has lost its hold on men. But what has come into its place but anti-art, just as there is anti-philosophy, anti-theatre and so on? It testifies to the fact that art is in a deep crisis" (pp. 194-195).

Rookmaaker suggests that advertising may be more interesting. Art that uses forms from industry, say, metal tubes or blocks, simply divests them of the meaning they originally had in the context of their function. He comes back to the question: What are people looking for? Of course, he concludes that there are no answers in the world's art: "One day we see that we are alone after all, and nothing has changed" (p. 209). He disappoints those who think it will all work out in the end, and that we really are making progress towards the ideal. He says there is no foundation to modern life, that people have just accepted the rhetoric of progress.

Thus there is protest, by people who are seeking more than a bland but safe life. Rookmaaker puts his faith in faith, the Christian path. The rest of the book sets out the Christian creed as the only foundation of a fulfilled life. I have been down that road. To follow it, one has to accept a creed, and it is like the box that surrounds the pope in Bacon's painting. Perhaps the cover art is appropriate. The end of it is a silent scream.

Did I need to examine this issue again? I was certainly not able to critique it at the time. And since then I have moved a long way. For a start, I began to think that it was inappropriate that Christianity claimed pre-eminence from all other religions when the Christians who were expounding the position were entirely ignorant of other religions and cultures. To be blunt, its creed condemned them and all their believers to Hell. This started to seem ridiculous as well as high-handed.

Later, I was introduced to the perspective that Christianity was primarily about belief, and it gives rise to arguments about belief. The interesting thing, as it turns out, is that the atheistic opponents likewise have arguments, because they have a contrary set of beliefs.

However, a third perspective arises that says, in living life, have regard to how you live your life. From Buddhism we get the idea that one improves one's life by living in peace and tranquillity, through meditation, discipline, love, and non-judgement.

Another way of putting it is this: the cost of having certainty about 'God' is that you have to strip the idea down to something that is tangible and manageable. An example of this is at work in Rookmaaker's book. Everything in art has to be corralled into schools and their orientation to the Chrisitan creed. The Christian has to have the final say. From this perspective, Andy Warhol is not just having fun (or anything else) when he paints a Campbell's tomato soup can; he is expressing the angst of a person who does not have Christianity.

Have we shifted from 1970? One answer to that question is 'No', because there is no 'we'. We have had punk rock and progressive rock. There is no progression here, for example, one as a reaction to the other. Rather, people are in different places and so they have different things to express. The overriding impression of Rookmaaker's book is judgement: we (the Christians) judge others (although perhaps not all Christians agreed with his perspective).

Originally, I didn't spend a lot of time with this book. I think I felt that I didn't quite agree with it, but I couldn't express why. I didn't have enough experience or understanding. Now I think that it sucked everything into its vortex and spat out judgements; that was the only purpose of the art – to stand for or against Christianity.

Have I read any books that offer a more worthwhile view? Well, not on art. I am still no expert, and do not aim to be. I enjoy looking at art; I am not so skilled at drawing conclusions from it. One of the artists mentioned by Rookmaaker is Kandinsky. Wassily Kandinsky (born 1866) was a Russian painter. According to Wikipedia, he is generally credited as being one of the pioneers of abstraction in western art. A show of his work has just started at the Art Gallery of New South Wales (November 2023).

I have seen images of some of Kandinsky's work, and I think he will be good to see. Rookmaaker considers him favourably, perhaps because early on he criticised materialism: "We must destroy the soulless, materialistic life of the nineteenth century, and build the life of the soul and the spirit of the twentieth century". After he embraced abstract art, Kandinsky painted life as essentially geometric, although he saw life as the irrationality of the rational, and bristling with menace. We shall see.

Have I read any books that offer a different perspective on religion? Well, many, but in the context of the current discussion, there is *After Atheism*, by Mark Vernon, published in 2007. So, I think it may take a long time before one is prepared to go right back to the beginning. Vernon says "something has gone wrong with modern religion in its forgetfulness of the unknowability of God, and the centrality of silence" (p. 141). As if to emphasise the point, there is a Glossary at the back of the book, and the explanation for 'God' is '[silence]'.

For Vernon, agnosticism is a position that respects the uncertainty that is integral to life. However, while this might be an acceptable position to take, it is still grounded in the pre-eminence of belief. It seems to miss the shift in thinking that comes in the wake of modern physics that recognises the centrality of energy, in contrast to the objective perspective of Newtonian matter. One book that sheds light on what this different perspective might look like is very recent, 2023.

Rick Rubin, a sound engineer who has worked with many music groups who have achieved world prominence, wrote the book, *The Creative Act: A Way of Being*. It is a book that is not centred on beliefs, but on being. Regardless of one's mental propositions about reality, there is awareness, practice, discipline, listening, understanding the phases of the creative process, the learning of techniques in that process, and cultivation of helpful habits.

There is an acceptance of the energy of life, a willingness to be open to the new, and likewise a willingness to shed the ego. All this is possible without a rigorous, concrete definition of God. Instead, we are part of all this. As an aside, it can be said that morality arises out of this approach to creativity, because it is what is in harmony with the nature of reality. And, one is tempted to look for parallels between Rubin and indigenous people.

### 28. The Invitation

By Oriah Mountain Dreamer, published 1999.

Like most people, I came across this text because someone showed it to me. If I think about all the special texts I have come across, there are a few, but it's not a huge number. There is Jesus' Sermon on the Mount ("Come unto me all ye who travail and are heavy-laden"), there is Paul's hymn to love ("Though I speak with the tongues and men and angels, but have not love…"). In the Old Testament there is the twenty-third psalm ("The Lord is my shepherd…"). There is *The Prophet* by Kahlil Gibran ("Then a woman said, Speak to us of joy and sorrow. And he answered: Your joy is your sorrow unmasked)", and there is St Francis of Assisi ("Lord, make me an instrument of Thy peace").

*The Invitation* was, in a similar way, exalted, and on first encounter it stopped me short. It was confronting. It seemed to be saying (whoever it was), "Life can be tough, but you have the strength to do whatever must be done." Not many people speak like that to you. Do I know anyone at all who ever spoke to me like that? This person is not a friend, they are above me; not God, but a teacher, a mentor, or wise guide.

"It doesn't interest me what you do for a living. I want to know what you ache for." Straight away, this text (Poem? Hymn? Proclamation? Invitation?) is taking away something you might think is of central importance in your life, and says that there is something more important. And that you know this! She asks (because, let's say, the voice is speaking through the author) if you are really living, or whether you have given up because you have been hurt. She asks whether you are willing to feel the hurt, because life is all of it, not just the nice bits.

You could say it is a hymn for when all your victories have vanished but the moon still shines on the lake – and asks you to dance. It is a hymn for the life you summon up then.

Some people I admire praised the book that this verse became. Wayne Dyer said "Her words pierced my shell." John O'Donohue said "A remarkable book, a fierce and tender presence. Its wisdom could become a lifelong companion."

The introduction to *The Invitation* says that "We live in a world of endless small talk, constant traffic jams, and overburdened schedules", and the book is a response to that. But since 1995, when the book was first published, it could also be said that we live in a world that is swamped in self-help tomes, and how does one avoid drowning in the swamp? Yes, some of those books might be good (that is, helpful to you), but many of them seem to be fatuous and glib.

*The Invitation* itself has generated a great deal of 'traffic'. One might say, "Beware of followers!" And perhaps the author was. She seems to have disappeared from sight. I found a website for her, with a blog, but the last entry is January 2021. Not that it matters. When you write a book, it is released from you, and hopefully people will find it to be something worthwhile – entertaining, valuable, helpful, funny – whatever the appropriate attribute is. There is no obligation on the author to repeat the feat and augment it.

J.D. Salinger seems to have followed this philosophy. After *The Catcher in the Rye* was released in 1951, there has been practically nothing from him, although the book unleashed a never-ending stream of mail from readers. But the book is the book. He never claimed to be a counsellor or to have anything to add to it. As Oriah

Mountain Dreamer said, "You have to be prepared to disappoint another to be true to yourself."

Oriah Mountain Dreamer is not her birth name. Does it seem like a strange name? Is she being pretentious? Criticism springs quickly to many people. On her website I read that she had a dream where a group of grandmotherly women suggested that she should take the name 'Oriah'. Soon after, she met a shaman who gave her the name "Mountain Dreamer". The shaman said it means "one who likes to find and push the edge". That's the story.

She is Canadian, if that helps. She would say it doesn't. She wrote "The Invitation" (the prose poem, as she calls it) late one night after a party, as a reaction to having been immersed in inconsequential small-talk. From there it went into a newsletter she sent to people who had been students of her workshops over the years. It was just at the time when the internet was birthing. From that initial group it leaked out to the world. Some years later, she received an email from a woman in Africa who said she had heard it read out at a meeting of a United Nations organisation.

She received word that it had been to New Zealand, England, South Africa, Rumania, the United States, and even Iceland. Then a publisher sent her a request from an author to use it at the front of her book, and the publisher invited her to write her own book based on "The Invitation". So, it became published and widely known.

Oriah said that the pattern of "The Invitation" was based on an exercise that David Whyte did in a workshop she had attended. David Whyte is another writer whom I admire. "It doesn't interest me.... I want to know...." It is a willingness to be honest and open, most of all, with yourself.

One of the things I like about *The Invitation* is that it does not set up a perfect world, or a world of the perfect 'spiritual' human. We may have a peaceful persona in place that we feel is real, and then something brings us undone. So, the question is, what is it that brings us undone? She gives us the assurance that the world is a mess, and this is where we have to live, but that living well is the very thing that is possible, living with uprightness and joy.

Oriah has written other books, but not too many. She wrote a book on creativity that I found worth reading (*What We Ache For*). *The Invitation* is the kind of book that I like to have more than one copy of, because then I have one to give away to a friend or acquaintance who might find it helpful. Accordingly, I bought it at the book fair, but when I got home, I discovered that I must have already given my other copy away.

Dare I say it: I think there is wisdom in there, for all that there is resistance to calling anyone wise. It seems too presumptuous. But I did not call her wise. I think there is wisdom in the book, and she would appreciate that distinction, for sometimes a writer finds that what they have just written is wiser than they are.

Thinking of the passages I mentioned at the start of this section, does one ask whether the writer has any other passages or books? Perhaps. What else did Jesus say? (Of course.) Or St Francis of Assisi? Or Kahlil Gibran? I laugh to think that I did find another book of Kahlil Gibran's that I didn't know about, at a later book fair.

I have always been wary of putting books in the foreground, because the object is not the books themselves. It is what they speak of; it is what they reveal or enable. As Oriah Mountain Dreamer says in *The Invitation*: "It doesn't interest me where or what or with whom you have studied. I want to know what sustains you, from the inside, when all else falls away."

## 29. The Road Less Travelled

By M. Scott Peck, published in 1978.

I have ventured already through a great many books, and at the same time it is only a small fraction of what is in the library. However, one cannot concentrate on all of the books in one's library at the same time, so my current method is a pathway. Is it a pathway that goes somewhere? Perhaps it will take us everywhere. In the spirit of Oriah Mountain Dreamer, wherever it takes us, if we really go, we will be the first person on that road.

Scott Peck's book is a road less travelled for me, because I was otherwise engaged at the time. It came out in America in 1978 and gradually became famous over the next five years. However, by then I had shifted my location and also my reference groups. I had disengaged from Christian groups, I had left Sydney, I had left teaching. I had become a father, and I was living on bush property outside of Kyogle, in the hills on the far north coast of New South Wales. I was immersed in an alternative lifestyle and trying to make my living in the bush.

I had no idea how to do that, despite the passion. In the end, I took a job at a local Catholic school, teaching mathematics, technical drawing and manual/technical arts. I kept a large garden at home, and I was renovating my house. I wasn't reading very much of anything; maybe *Earth Garden* magazine, that's all. Occasionally I would visit a bookshop in Lismore, "Noah's Arc" (not 'Ark'). Scott Peck's book arrived there, I think. It was a new Age bookshop, but *The Road Less Travelled* was sufficiently "left of centre" for it to be accepted there.

I think I felt that I was myself on a road less travelled (living in a 1930s dairy farmer's house in a valley where the road eventually petered out), and it was probably parallel to his life in some way, but it wasn't necessary for me to explore his road. I had my hands full. Besides, it seemed that he was a Christian, and hadn't I left that behind me, despite my job in a Catholic school?

Strangely, about ten years later, I was in another job, as the manager of an organisation that ran several services for people with intellectual disabilities, and I ran into a cess pit of trouble. I found myself in the midst of an unseemly battle for the survival of the organisation and its assets, orchestrated by the distant head office in Sydney. They were going to destroy our local branch and take the assets to fund a fight they were wanting to have with the Federal Government.

It was accompanied by the most dishonest and nasty behaviour imaginable, targeting me. I was eventually sacked and had to make radical changes to my life. I ended up coming back to Sydney to live. It took me twenty-five years to finally write down what happened. It became my first novel (based on true life): *The Ten Thousand Things*.

What was strange that involved Scott Peck? Only this incident. When the fight was at its worst, and I was in the midst of it, and getting ostracised by people in my own town because they had been told lies about me, I went down to Byron Bay for the weekend. I went into a bookshop, not with a purpose, but just to browse. The night before, I had had a dream about a snake, a snake I understood to be poisonous and ready to kill.

I was walking down the aisles of the bookshop, pulling a book out now and then to look at it, when I pulled out a book and there was a picture of a snake. It was a chilling moment. The title of the book was *People of the Lie*, and the author was M. Scott Peck. I had to buy the book and read it.

The people I was dealing with in this vile battle were exactly like some of the portraits in that book. Invariably, they were cold and calculating, and had no compunction about doing wrong, lying, or causing harm; in my case, even to people with disabilities. It was merely how you managed to get what you wanted. This was a revelation to me. Were there people like that? Of course, when you are reading history, you encounter people like that, but in ordinary life? It was a shock to me, and I had to admit I was naïve.

I didn't have to lose my principles, but I had to recognise that there were people who did not share them. In that sense, I had to toughen up. So, I lost my job (I was sacked) and the nasty people (I know, crude language, but it was true) tried to dismantle most of what I had built up over six years, but there was a point at which they did not get what they wanted. I had Scott Peck to thank for hauling me out of a helpless depression. I acquired some of the qualities of a warrior.

There is another twist in the tale of Scott Peck's books. At the book fair, I thought that I had acquired *The Road Less Travelled* at an earlier book fair (although I still hadn't read it), so I didn't buy the copy there. The truth was, the book I had bought was *The Different Drum*. I had been thinking I should give up my resistance to Scott Peck. But I still hadn't read that book. To be fair, I always have a long reading list.

In the end, I resorted to buying a copy of *The Road Less Travelled* at an online book site, because I was still interested in seeing what it had to say. (This was one of the two books that arrived in my letterbox after having been left at the wrong address down the road.) When I finally sat down to read it, I was immediately wary. The book signalled early on that the author believed in God, and that psychotherapists have some special powers to understand human life, and to interpret yours for you. I was unsettled. My copy of the book (which contained the introduction to the 25th anniversary edition) said the book had been purchased by ten million people. Nevertheless.

The book begins with the statement "Life is difficult." Part 1 of the book is called 'Discipline' (followed by Love, Growth and Religion, and Grace). Compare: "It doesn't interest me what you do for a living. I want to know what you ache for, and if you dare to dream of meeting your heart's longing" (Oriah Mountain Dreamer). Or, "Be impeccable with your word" (Don Miguel Ruiz).

I am always suspect when the first thing a prophet, or evangeliser, says is something that preys on your supposed misery. What if the first thing you've got to say is "It's a wonderful world", à la Louis Armstrong? Even despite everything else that might be going on. Shouldn't our starting point be: It's a wonderful world?

The next proposition from Scott Peck is that people mostly try to avoid trouble, problems and difficulties, and that causes neurosis. I object to this move. This is a medicalised perspective on life. Who would do that? Oh yes, a psychotherapist. Later in the book, he warns that ordinary people should not try to conduct psychotherapy; that's for professionals. It's ironic that one of the chapters is on dependency. I am not being glib.

Perhaps it is that, as a psychotherapist, Scott Peck is only dealing with the most wounded of people. Certainly, some of the case stories he presents are extreme. Why do this? One suggestion is that he sees miracles at work here, so it is only a short step from the stories to religion. However, years ago I learned the distinction between magic and spirituality. To use my words, one is about performance, and the other is about soul. I use the word 'miracle' sparingly, because too often it just means magic, and then we simply end up in a fight with the scientists. Spirituality (soul) gets left aside.

I thought there was some potentially useful material in Scott Peck's book. He has a chapter on "Taking time to solve problems", which is essentially about taking the time that is needed to understand a problem so that you can figure out how to solve it. However, for some more far-reaching advice I would go to the Four Agreements, where it says: "Don't take anything personally, and don't make assumptions." I think these really are skills that are worth learning and practising, and they are not easy.

I had reservations about many of the examples he used. I thought his interpretations simply betrayed his perspective rather than being convincing. At one point he describes an episode between himself and his daughter. She was conscientious at school, and he felt that she should "loosen up" and be more flexible. And he thought that he should spend more time with her, and she liked chess, so one night he invited her to play chess.

She agreed, but then wanted to go to bed after a while, because she had to get up early for school. He insisted that she continue to play, in an effort to teach her to be more flexible about the time she went to bed. But his daughter just got more and more upset. And then, Scott Peck, the author, saw his daughter as being at fault rather than himself. Reading this, I wasn't against his far aim, to teach his daughter flexibility, but it seemed obvious to me that his behaviour was insensitive and even disrespectful. And why use an example that was so suspect? Was he that sure of himself? I was disenchanted.

Scott Peck advocates that we live a life of "stringent self-examination". To my mind, that is a lean offering. One can sense the stern parent in the background, perhaps even the weight of the (American) society behind it. Contrast that with the approach of the Dalai Lama, who is asking how we are faring in the quest for happiness, and suggests that having compassion for others would be helpful. Or the approach of Oriah Mountain Dreamer, who says, "I want to know what you ache for."

Can Scott Peck help us with a definition of love? One would like to think so. He says: "Love is the will to extend oneself for the purpose of nurturing one's own or another's spiritual growth" (p. 83). I found this confusing. Surely, love is kind? It is hard to read kindness into Scott Peck's definition. If someone drops a parcel, and their hands are full, and I pick up the parcel and hand it back to them, there is no notion of spiritual growth for either party, except in a vague, convoluted way. It is merely an act of kindness and, to that extent, love.

The chapter in the New Testament where Paul praises love says "Love suffers long and is kind; love does not envy; love does not parade itself, is not puffed up" (I Corinthians 13: 4). It is hard to see how any of this is "for the purpose of nurturing spiritual growth". There is no purpose; one performs kindness with clean hands.

What does Scott Peck mean? The example he uses is the patient who said his mother really loved him because she wouldn't let him get the bus to school by himself until he was in his teens. Scott Peck is saying that if the mother had let him get the bus, it would have been for the purpose of his spiritual growth. But in framing his definition of love this way, he has distorted the essence of it, and for this proposition I reference the Bible.

In the book there is a great deal of concern for science and its interaction with religion. However, I think the conceptions of both science and religion are, at best, outmoded. A discussion of them would not be helpful. Scott Peck talks about worldviews in maintaining that "everyone has a religion". However, I think that this move extracts any useful meaning out of both words. I think that at this point, we are talking about Scott Peck's worldview rather than anything else.

I was left feeling that the book constructed a philosophy of social conformism, in which there was little thought of joy or creativity. I was disappointed with it. I felt as if I was one of the many people who bought the book to see what it was saying. This is how a book goes from being popular to being a best-seller.

Lastly, why did the author call the book "The road less travelled"? Maybe it's obvious: of all the people in society, many will choose not to think about the things in this book, that is, about discipline, avoidance of responsibility, growth, love, religion, and grace. But the model held up in the book is about people learning lessons that presumably everyone should learn, or need to learn in order to grow up. I would not have promoted this as the road less travelled. One would hope that it becomes the broad road, although I suspect that

Scott Peck sees the path as the narrow road that leads to Heaven, as opposed to the broad road that leads to destruction (Matthew 7:13).

## 30. The New Chinese Astrology
By Suzanne White, published 1993.

This book turned up at the book fair, and I knew I had bought it (at another book fair) a few years ago. I am not dismissive of astrology, Chinese or Western, and I have looked at it. I simply haven't felt that it validated itself for me. In Chinese astrology I am a Tiger. Your sign is not based on the month you were born, as in Western astrology. Rather, it is based on the year you were born, on a twelve-year cycle. The twelve signs are animals: rat, ox, tiger, cat, dragon, snake, horse, goat, monkey, rooster, dog, pig.

Each animal has certain qualities, and you should be able to recognise them in your personality. It could be useful to know this, because it might explain why you are the way you are. It might also explain how you get on with certain other people or not, because some animals get on with each other and some don't.

The Chinese signs have been in use for several thousand years. They came into popularity around 2900 BCE, which was the time of the Emperor, Fu Hsi. They were codified over time, and were adopted officially in 2637 BCE. Fu Hsi is also credited with the invention of the eight trigrams of the I Ching, which were later combined into hexagrams with accompanying commentary. Although this date is precise, Fu Hsi is a legendary character. Not that it matters; there were scholars who studied such things and compiled the literature.

Suzanne White says, "I am amazed by the uncanny accuracy of Chinese astrology". Oh, if I could but see it! Am I noble and fearless, respected for my courage and dreaded for my ferocity? Am I like a raging torrent? Am I in such a hurry? Am I so impetuous? Do I rush into battles with relish?

I cannot identify myself in this picture. It gets harder: my favourite colour is red; my flower is the carnation; jasmine for perfume; my flavour is sweet; lucky number is seven; fruit is fruit pie; metal is gold; herb is thyme; musical instrument is the trumpet.

I do not find any of this helpful, not a single thing. Although, do people seriously have lucky numbers and favourite colours anyway?

The "terrible tiger" is a doer, a mover, a shaker, and an accomplisher of world-class projects. We are attracted by his magical aura, enthralled by his charm, enchanted and impressed by his fun-filled lifestyle. There are several pages of this description. I read it all, but I was just as mystified at the end as I was at the beginning.

Perhaps Suzanne White sees the qualities in people that she talks about, and can correlate it all with their birth dates. But my single criterion is: is it helpful? How could I find this helpful. I read one comment that said: "I didn't think I exhibited a particular quality, but when I asked my mother, she gave me some examples, and then I could see it."

However, I do not think that my mother, or any of my friends, past or present, have ever seen me as "a mover and a shaker". I might achieve goals, but the personality described here is like Tigger in *Winnie the Pooh*, forever bouncing around with excess energy. It is not me. I would like to see more in this book than I have; I am not philosophically opposed to it.

However, not should one try over-hard to fit oneself into a mould. That would fly in the face of the book's avowed aim: to enable you to see and recognise yourself. Why do we try to see ourselves in a hall of portraits: totem animals or astrological signs? I suppose it is an extension of being recognised by our parents, carers and other members of our families when we are young.

We abstract it out to a generic picture; it is some form of identification in the wider world. It connects us with others, whom we presume ourselves to be like, and it places us in a larger landscape, where everyone has a place: one of the twelve signs of the zodiac or the twelve animals of the Chinese horoscope. Suzanne

White also introduces the five elements (earth, metal, water, wood, fire), so I am a Wood Tiger. And she lists famous people who were Wood Tigers. Some of the ones whose names I recognised were: Princess Anne, Phil Collins, Mel Gibson, William Hurt. I could choose to see myself in these people, but I don't.

The system also places us in time. The day we were born, even the hour and the minute, as well as the place, are significant. I think they are, because your conception and birth began the chain of events which is your life. The underlying truth of it, however, is not so simple to determine. To say I am a Gemini Tiger is merely to cast at something. Occasionally it might even function as an excuse; you should expect no more or less of such a person.

It is also a substitute for understanding, like a way-station on the way to a destination. We may not have arrived, but it's a good place to stay for a cup of tea and a sandwich. It will do for now.

I think the same of other tools for mapping humans. The Myers-Briggs Type Indicator (MBTI) is very popular. The DiSC personality profile is also popular (dominance, influence, steadiness, and conscientiousness). The Big Five personality test is another (its dimensions are openness to experience, conscientiousness, extraversion, agreeableness, and neuroticism). And there is the Enneagram, which has a history of around 2,000 years.

These are all tools that can be used to explore the dimensions of oneself. Perhaps the same question arises in each case (including astrology here as well): the avenue may provide some new perceptions about oneself, but what does one do with this knowledge? Does it constitute material that one can work on? I may see myself as too impetuous, too dominant, not open enough to experience.... Or, does it become an excuse not to change?

Do you formulate goals or rules for yourself, and make an effort to follow them?

At a higher level, how does your view of the human world change? How do your values change? How does your awareness change? It may give us a measure of peace to see ourselves reflected in one or more of these frameworks, and it may inspire us to want to evolve.

Sometimes we have to immerse ourselves in a book or tool for a while, even if we are not sure whether it will hold any value. We have to suspend judgement. Later, we may have to step outside again and see if our efforts are proving worthwhile. Ultimately comes the hard question: is it worth my spending my time on this? And we can ask ourselves, what insights, feelings or resolutions have come of it?

In these modern days, we also have to be prepared to step around fluff. In the 2020 edition of White's book, the marketing calls it "a classic work of writing genius" that will enable you "to find out who you are". It claims that the book explains "why people's behaviour is *pre-determined* by their Chinese Horoscope" (my emphasis). The core competency of many marketers today is over-reach.

In the copy I have, White is much more modest. She doesn't make any of the above claims. She says she learned from an old Chinese gentleman (I don't doubt her), and she simply says she hopes the book will help you. She wasn't well-known when she wrote the book. Success breeds its own little industry around the writer.

## 31. Intuition

By Paul Fenton-Smith, published 2011.

Always there is the question: why is this book at the book fair? Was it because the former owner was displeased with the book, or had they felt that someone else should get a chance to read it? One never knows. There is always that ambiguity. This is a beautifully made book, not a cheap trade paperback. One would think seriously about moving it off your bookshelf.

This book was interesting for the way it came to me. I did not buy it; it was given to me. I worked as the editor at a magazine, and occasionally people would send us books to review. They weren't always suitable. In this case, the book was given to our marketing manager, even though it seemed to be felt that it would not be suitable for the magazine. The marketing manager thought I might like the book, personally, and gave it to me. We agreed that we couldn't put a review of the book into the magazine.

I read the book at my leisure. The sub-title is "Keys to unlocking your inner wisdom". I am accustomed to being surrounded by pragmatic, rationalistic people, and this seems to be the way of the world, inescapably. But intuitive information can arrive in your mind as a flash of inspiration, a creative idea, a hunch about a situation, an impression of a person when you first meet them, or through strong dreams at night.

The book was suggesting that it could assist us to discover our intuitive strengths and improve our psychic abilities as we seek to find our path in life. It could help us, not only to be more creative and more successful, but to live a happier life. It set out a path of psychic development which leads to spiritual fulfilment. It would mean being able to recognise all of the viable avenues for nourishment and development, and feeling that we have plentiful reserves of spiritual energy.

"Life can be a powerful distraction from your purpose. It offers temptations that seem like shortcuts." The offerings of the book are set out in terms of two keys, one gold and one silver. The gold key represents the processes, techniques, doctrines and rules (for example, meditation). The silver key represents the mystery behind the processes, the inner state of the person: being calm, centred and content.

The author holds that we are able to increase our intuition if we give attention to it, through exercises and practices. He talks about meditation as a way of getting centred, and he discusses the importance of being centred. It is common for people today to be hectic and scattered, and this is debilitating, especially over the long term.

Does he recommend that we find a master to be our guide? No, he doesn't. He says we are each able to find our own path up the mountain. A master is someone who has been up the mountain and can be a guide, but it is not essential. He also says that we should go within, quietly, to consider whether things we have been told by others are true or helpful for us. There is discipline in this life, but one should be wary of severity.

He talked about psychic protection. When we move among many people every day, some of whom carry anger, sadness, confusion and other negative feelings, whether or not they are consciously directed towards us, we pick up the vestiges of those feelings. It causes us confusion and despondency in turn. It is good to be aware of this and to cleanse ourselves regularly. He recommends meditation, breathing, bathing, spending time in nature, swimming, and devising our own centring rituals.

I think that a book like this needs to be taken in small, simple steps. I, for example, am shaped by my everyday environment, and it is challenging to think of the unseen world of energy. Yet we know the inklings of intuition, and it makes sense that these inklings can be strengthened for our benefit.

Some of the book is about developing various psychic skills, and some people might consider using these skills professionally.

There is, however, a much broader sense in which intuition is relevant to all of us. From another book in my library, Richard Rudd's *Gene Keys*, comes the thought: our modern society cultivates an atmosphere of anxiety, and it is within this that we live. Without effort we participate in this unease (think of Fenton-Smith's assertion of the need for psychic cleaning). One result is that society invests a great deal of effort into seeking to safeguard our security and safety. However, the fear is not outside; it is in the mind, so it is pervasive.

The reason for the emphasis on centring and meditation is that they give rest to the mind, and bring calm to the body. Then we may participate in the peace, and open the way for intuition. We may hear what comes on the wind. "Intuition is our body's system for interacting harmoniously in the world." Intuition achieves things through harmony instead of through force of mind. We need to learn to trust our intuition again, to listen, and to feel physically at ease. (Rudd, Chapter 57)

This approach helped me to fit Fenton-Smith's work on intuition into a wider framework, instead of seeing the skills he mentioned as arbitrary, special and randomly distributed. I suppose it is the silver key.

## 32. The Element

By Ken Robinson, published 2009.

I acquired Ken Robinson's book at a book fair in recent years. It was a question of finding something that I knew about. The sub-title of the book is "How finding your passion changes everything". Is it a "New Age" book? No, he doesn't fit into that category. Or does he? If the world had no walls, he could be standing shoulder to shoulder with people of that ilk.

I came across Robinson in an unexpected place: a national conference on human resources, perhaps in Sydney, and it was probably in 2009, which was the year that this book was published. (I have surveyed my shelf of notebooks, and found notes that I took at his session; it was in June 2009.) I used to work for a company that provided information resources for human resource managers (and lawyers, accountants and the like). I used to write commentary and articles about topics in employment law, human resources and training and development.

Once a year a group of about five of us would go to the human resources conference, and write articles about what we heard. They were published the following week online. We reported on new ideas and innovations in management and training. Ken Robinson was an unusual choice as the keynote speaker, because he was not directly related to the human resources 'industry', whether as an academic, practitioner, or as a company executive. He was from the educational sphere.

However, his message was applicable to industry. He was saying that the world is changing rapidly, and employers are saying they need workers who are creative, but the education system is squashing creativity out of students. Likewise, creativity in the workplace is undervalued and not encouraged. In the book, he argues that the future of humanity, its communities and institutions may depend on a new paradigm of human capacity.

I remember that he was truly engaging, and he spoke in a large auditorium of over a thousand people for an hour and a half, using only a few slides as props, and never losing the attention of his audience. He was passionate, articulate and illuminating. He had also earned his place in the public eye. In the late 1990s he had led a UK commission on creativity, education and the economy, and his report was received with acclaim. *The Times* said: "This report raises some of the most important issues facing business in the 21st century. It should have every CEO and human resources director thumping the table and demanding action."

The question for human resource managers was how they might go about nurturing talent in their organisation, bearing in mind that the education system has been educating people out of their creativity, with its emphasis on narrowly conceived subject matter and standardised tests. In the book, Robinson spelled out what is needed. We need to create environments where every person is inspired to grow creatively. Part of this is to ensure that every person has the chance to do what they should be doing – and he spells out how such an environment can be fostered.

*The Element* explains what the element is: the experience of personal talent meeting personal passion. Or, "what I am good at" meets "what I care about, and am interested in". He argues that in this encounter, we feel most ourselves, most inspired, and we achieve to our highest level.

Robinson maintains that people have very diverse talents; they are not all the same, so a standardised model is not effective. He argues against a mechanistic, industrial approach to education and training. The fostering of creativity is more like farming, because the growth of creativity is organic. So, like the farmer, all you can do is create the conditions under which it will begin to flourish. People will find what they love to do.

Most people have not found their element. They simply fulfil their job in a routine way, detached from their work. But it is essential to the well-being and ultimate success of individuals that they find their element. And it is essential for organisations to find ways to enable their people to find their element. By implication, this endeavour is essential to the health of our organisations and our society.

He suggests that our current patterns of work and behaviour are embedded in us through frameworks of ideas and beliefs: the idea that it is not possible to allow people to be creative, that that is not how the world works. There is also a mechanistic model of the universe lurking behind the things people say and do. But it is this mechanistic thinking, categorising things and separating them mentally, that has led to our disastrous issues with the climate. We don't see that things are organic and connected, and that they affect each other.

Having a large population on earth, and having so many people congregated in cities, makes all of our problems critical. We can no longer ignore them. Mental health problems like depression and suicide are part of the whole system that we live within. Fostering creativity lies at the root of improving the whole system. He urges us to find the element within ourselves, and to enable others to find it and use it.

It is interesting that the element is not a material thing. Rather, it is an atmosphere: "they are in their element". I think that is an extraordinary fact. If you were to look for that, you would be looking for the thing that you do well and that you enjoy doing. You would be looking out for that feeling. Then, you would want to recreate those conditions.

Life is often not so kind. Our socio-economic circumstances might lead us in other directions. But there is also persistence and ingenuity that might help us to shift our circumstances. There is also choice about jobs, homes, relationships, choices that might move us closer to where we think we need to be in order to be in our element.

Robinson tells the story of Matt Groening, the creator of *The Simpsons*. He knew that he liked drawing cartoons, but he thought that he would have to get a boring job (his image was, working in a tyre warehouse), then draw cartoons in his spare time. He had a cartoon published in a small magazine, then was interviewed to work at a studio, and he pitched the idea for *The Simpsons* off the top of his head. It bore long-term fruit.

There are many stories of people, creativity and success. The stories are as different as people are. Ken Robinson was prominent because he had a world-wide impact on the conversation about creativity, society and education. What he said resonated with me because I had been a schoolteacher, and I had felt stultified by the system. No matter; I never felt that I was in my element in the classroom, but I did feel that it could be a better place.

Robinson said that the purpose of education was to enable children to find their element and to cultivate it. In small ways, many teachers try. However, the more that schools become bureaucratised (and 'accountable'), the more pressure there is to narrow the syllabus to the subjects "that employers want" and to standardise testing. The overlay is that educational systems are always trying to minimise the cost of marking, so testing is steered towards technology-facilitated means.

It is not so much a question of testing for understanding; it is a question of testing the things that can be easily tested. It is a very high-level skill to generate multiple-choice questions (for example) that actually require sharpened understanding.

I feel that Ken Robinson would have appreciated Rick Rubin's book on creativity. Robinson died in 2020, and Rubin's book was published in 2023. But it is admittedly easier to talk about a system or method you intend to apply to yourself, and quite another to formulate a system to regulate the lives of thousands, or millions, of people. Or even an amenable system at the organisational level.

However, Robinson talks about understanding human motivation, and if the leaders of the organisation, school, university or system have a decent understanding of that, there is scope for something good to be created. It may be more important to clarify the organisation's operational (that is, real rather than rhetorical) values than to make methods rigorous. It is a question of finding congenial mental models; the farmer model is more appropriate than the factory model.

It is possibly hazardous to look for books at book fairs that reflect what you already own. Perhaps the books that turn up will not be relevant any longer. It is some years since I was working in a job writing content for organisational professionals. I no longer think in terms of what initiatives might be productive in an organisation. But Ken Robinson's book demonstrates that principles may persist.

From my notes from the 2009 conference, I had picked up Robinson's emphasis on being "in your element". He used the example of Eric Clapton, the rock guitarist, to illustrate the marriage of aptitude and love, and the resulting burst of imagination. He also emphasised that following this path leads you in unpredictable directions. You cannot impose a linear narrative on your life. He finished with a reference to W.B. Yeats, the Irish poet, and the importance he afforded to dreams. A life of passion, living in "the element", gives fire to imagination and allows room for dreams.

His ideas may have been articulated in 2009, but they have been woven into societal conversations since then, and people like Rick Rubin have taken the ideas further: the next steps.

### 33. Being Mortal

By Atul Gawande, published 2014.

I was surprised to see this book, because it was a fairly recent discovery of mine. It was hard to imagine that someone else had similarly discovered it, and already wanted to pass it on. But that is to forget that the former owner may have bought it soon after it was published, which was a few years ago now.

My reason for buying the book is funny. I am over seventy, and although I am well and healthy, I thought I should give some thought to death before it is, in a Shakespearean sense, fast upon me. It seems reasonable.

I am not close to death. I am not ill, and I am not bored. When I was sixty-eight, I went to England, and I was in a country church in Cornwall when I saw some cards on a rack. (It was at Towednack, where the Martin family came from nearly 170 years ago.) I had not yet left my job, but the thought was certainly in my mind.

The card was headed: "Retirement: A New Beginning". It said, "The Lord continue to extend your vision to widen your horizons; The Lord continue to awaken your senses, to deepen your experience, That you may enter new life and go forward in joy; That you have new ventures and continue to serve him in the power of the Almighty who makes all things new."

I thought, "Yes, exactly." I would not have included all the references to the Lord, but I understood the sentiment. I was never fearful of retirement because I never thought that I would ever retire, in the sense of downing tools and sitting on the porch every day. When I did leave work, I said I was in 'quasi-retirement'. I wrote four books in the next twelve months. Not that I had increased my workload; it was just that the books were there already, in the ether, and needed to be put into words, and I didn't have to go to the office every day.

So, what did Atul Gawande have to say, and why did I remember his name? I thought I must have bought another book by this person. It is a memorable name. But I haven't yet catalogued the books in my library, so there was no reason why I should be able to find the book. Perhaps Mister Gawande would recommend that I catalogue all my books as a retirement project.

And then I found the book. It was: *The Checklist Manifesto*. That was most unexpected. One expects an author to write the same kind of books. Although, I don't, so why would I think that?

The *Checklist* book was first: 2011, and the *Being Mortal* book was in 2014. So, he is a man who thinks about a lot of things. I investigated. He is a surgeon who lives in Boston, and he teaches at Harvard Medical School. He is younger than me by fifteen years, so one assumes he did not write the latter book on his death bed. So, he decided to think about it early as well, although doctors see a lot more of sickness and death than I do.

The *Checklist* book was about what strategies we could devise to avoid, or respond to, crises. He wasn't just thinking about medical emergencies. One of his examples is the Hurricane Katrina disaster in New Orleans in August 2005. He asks whether the public sector or the private sector is better at dealing with crises, but he says, that's not it.

It is a question of realising that we live in complex environments, and the knowledge required to deal with things exceeds what any individual can attain, including the leader, so centralisation of power and processes is not the answer. The answer is to have competent people and give them freedom, and to codify knowledge in checklists. The checklists ensure that important things are not overlooked, and they make accountability more possible.

Now Atul Gawande was turning his attention to the evening of life: "Illness, Medicine, and What Matters in the End" (the sub-title). He has testimonies from Malcolm Gladwell and Oliver Sacks. The *Sydney Morning Herald* called it "A fascinating blend of memoir, research, philosophy and personal encounters with patients.... He crafts precise, scalpel-sharp prose." (Yes, I could have left out the metaphor.) Peter Carey, an Australian author, called it "wise and courageous.... His concern and dedication shine from every page."

The context for the book is that advances in medicine over the last century have increased life expectancy so much that people (generally) have started to think they are going to live forever, and that they will not experience a decline in their powers, and perhaps an increase in their medical troubles, prior to death. He reminds us that up until the last 200 years, the average human life span was thirty years. In 2023 in Australia, it was 83.94 years. The latest figure for males was 81.2 and for females, 85.3.

Seen in this context, current life expectancy is remarkable. But my observation is that people still die. You may be able to take the book out from the library for a little longer, but you still have to take it back eventually. It is the library's book. So with your life. Cheerful rhetoric about long lives seems to miss the point. Moreover, there are many things that occur largely in youth: sporting prowess, youthful beauty, and mathematical breakthroughs. These do not persist into old age. If there are exceptions, then that is exactly what they are: exceptions.

Gawande is aware of these dimensions. He spends time describing how the body gradually breaks down or degenerates as we grow older: bones, skin, teeth, arteries, muscles, lungs, brain. His treatment is comprehensive. And, borrowing from his previous book, he says we are complex systems, so we don't break down simply. Parts of us may atrophy and the rest of us carries on as best it can.

In reading this book, I wanted to hold it up against others that I have read, for example, Deepak Chopra, Louise Hay, Bruce Lipton. Is Gawande giving a generic picture of people who are unreflective about their lives? Is he painting a blanket picture based on statistical averages? It would be a mistake to think that your life will necessarily follow the average.

I think of my parents. Father: died at fifty-three (heart attack); mother: died at ninety-three, although when younger, she thought she was going to die before she turned fifty. Me? I am seventy-three. My parents' parents? Father's father: seventy-two; father's mother: seventy-five. Mother's father: forty-nine; mother's mother: fifty-three. But Gawande then tells us that the correlation between the age of a person's death and that of their parents is only three percent.

Gawande quotes the warrior Karna in the Mahabharata: "I see it now – this world is swiftly passing". He has a chapter in his book called "Things fall apart". Somewhere in my library I have a book with that title. Ah yes: *When Things Fall Apart* by Pema Chodron.

Or, are the other books I mentioned books for younger people, books that are not cognisant of the age of "being aged"? At least Gawande is saying that old age is a legitimate period of life. The question is whether it is necessarily decrepit. I have had a chance to read Deepak Chopra's new book, *Living in the Light*. He is old now, but he has not slunk away to age in obscurity. What does he say? That life is about consciousness, and our task is to cultivate awareness – and practise yoga!

In so saying, Chopra is asserting that life is not about eternal appearance or the accumulation of power and dominance. He makes the bold statement: "Your true self is immune to fear, depression, aging and death." He presents this as a true core belief, the context being that there are beliefs that are common among people in society: that I don't matter, that life is unfair, that I need to look out for myself, that the universe is cold and unloving, and the forces of nature are all-powerful.

Chopra says, what is at stake here is reality. Your beliefs pertain to how you feel about reality. That is a radical statement. These are not provable propositions. The real question is: how do you feel about reality? He is recommending that we live in consciousness, that therein lies our grounding and our evolution, in the face of what life brings us.

What I got from Gawande's book was an acceptance of the need to accept my place in life, all the aspects of it, and especially the physical aspects of having a body in the world as the body grows older. But does Gawande accept the existence of a 'true self'? He talks about the need for humans to have something beyond themselves that they care about, drawing on a book published by an American philosopher in 1908.

This was a surprise. Most of Gawande's book consists of stories about aged people, their experience of life, and the contemporary aged care system and how it does not serve their human needs very well. A philosophy book from 1908 was not looming. Josiah Royce, a Harvard professor, was an "absolute idealist", believing that "all aspects of reality are ultimately unified in the thought of a single all-encompassing consciousness". The book was called *The Philosophy of Loyalty*.

It was Royce addressing himself to the ethical questions of human life. To lead a life of significance, one's actions must express a "self-consciously asserted will". As Gawande notes, simply being alive and safe is not enough. Given that most aged care facilities seem to have this as their only aim, Gawande is being critical. We need a cause beyond ourselves, even into old age. It could be broad: family, country, a principle, or it could be near: the care of another person, a pet, or a garden.

This is what Royce saw as loyalty. I have to insert the observation that I think loyalty is a very problematic value. Isn't loyalty something that the Mafia cultivates? And under that shadow, people can commit all kinds of crimes and sins. I am very careful in my use of the term 'loyalty' for this reason. It is what I call a subsidiary value: it needs to be in the service of greater principles.

However, Royce is more generous with the word. For him, it represents something we are prepared to forget ourselves for, or make sacrifices for. It is a cause that we develop commitment to. It does not necessarily produce happiness, but it demonstrates that we all need something more than ourselves to be devoted to. In contrast, our selfish desires are fleeting, capricious and insatiable, and ultimately they give us only torment.

Gawande concludes that the only way death is not meaningless is to see yourself as part of something greater. He quotes Royce: "Loyalty solves the paradox of our ordinary existence by showing us outside of ourselves the cause which is to be served, and inside of ourselves the will which delights to do this service, and which is not thwarted but enriched and expressed in such service" (p. 127).

While we may feel less urge for achievement as we grow older, that is, we are less ambitious, we become more concerned about our legacy. The medical industry and aged care institutions are focused on medical concerns but have almost no view of what makes life significant. As the number of aged people increases, and as they require more support, this distortion is becoming more marked. People also need, at the end, to be able to have conversations that recognise the inevitability of death, so that that passage can be undertaken with understanding and dignity.

Chopra says that to live with consciousness means that we cannot live in certainty. Life is unpredictable. Accordingly, we cannot make reliable plans for the future, but if we can set ego aside, our consciousness will evolve, day by day.

At the end of his book, Atul Gawande goes to the Ganges to spread the ashes of his father on the holy river: "After spreading his ashes, we floated silently for a while, letting the current take us. As the sun burned away the mist, it began warming our bones. Then we gave a signal to the boatman, and he picked up his oars. We headed back towards the shore" (p. 263).

In the end, we have to integrate all of it.

I have not delved into all the other books in my library in this exercise, but when I am in a topic, sometimes a book will call out. I bought another book on aging. I bought it in a bookstore, a bookstore I had not been to before, in Paddington, and I bought a book for the same reason you make an offering in a church. It is gratitude that the place is there as an offering to the community. It was Lewis Richmond, *Every Breath, New Chances: How to Age with Honour and Dignity, A Guide for Men* (2020).

I knew the writer and he interested me. But that's for another time. Writing a book is an exercise, and one must plan to get to the end of it at some point. This book is not the Great Work; it's just me talking to you. But I do know: In the end, we have to integrate all of it.

## 34. 488 Rules for Life

By Kitty Flanagan, published 2019.

Kitty Flanagan is a funny lady with a long career of stand-up comedy and roles in several amusing and incisive television series. The title of her book is a sarcastic dig at Jordan Peterson's book, *Twelve Rules for Life*. The title consists of hand-drawn block letters; '12' has been crossed out and replaced by '488'. The sub-title of her book is: "The Thankless Art of Being Correct".

I saw Kitty Flanagan live in May 2023, at the Enmore Theatre in Sydney. She was funny. What impresses me most, however, is the mere fact that a person can talk on stage non-stop for an hour and a half, and be both lucid and funny. I may be jealous. Moreover, she is not a sociopath, which is an occupational hazard for comedians. She is sharp, but she is not savage.

Years ago, I had the idea that I would think up titles for books and put them up on a website. The books would not exist. Then, I would see what reaction the various titles got, and if one was popular, I would write that book. The logistics of the exercise might have been problematic (people might say, "Where's my book?") but it was an interesting idea.

Flanagan beat me. She had a comedy sketch on a television show about this book, "488 Rules", as a spoof on Jordan Peterson, and afterwards people kept asking her where they could get the book. With encouragement like that, she did write the book. I have Peterson's book, and there are useful things in it, but he does leave you feeling uneasy. For example, there is a rule for which there is a long story about Adam and Eve and the Garden of Eden, and I was left with the question, "So, is he a Creationist? Is he trying to persuade me to be a Creationist?"

At the end of the book there was the question, was that worth my time? And, is there a sub-text here? What is he really trying to say? And then he seemed to get co-opted by some rather crazy people, and in the end it wasn't clear whether or not he was one of them.

I don't have that problem with Kitty Flanagan. Let's start at the beginning: "Rule 1: If you don't agree with a rule, forget about it and move on to the next one." So, we learn straightaway that she is a tolerant person, and not too self-obsessed. I like that.

"Rule 2: Football jerseys are not art." Ah, so this is going to be a practical book. Don't frame football jerseys and hang them on the wall. This is in the "General House Rules" section. Some people might argue that football jerseys are not art; they are memorabilia, and therefore valid. That may be a justifiable point. In thinking about this, and after having been through the whole book, I think I have a fairly clear picture of the types of men who would not be her boyfriend. It starts with Rule 2.

"Rule 3: Don't waste your money on surround sound." She explains this by saying it is actually creepy for the voices of people and the sound of footsteps to be coming from behind you when the image is on the screen in front of you. I feel a glimmer of camaraderie. I am not the only one to have thought this.

Mostly, Kitty's rules are about human pretentions, laziness, and selfishness. "Rule 26: Cushions are not spiritual advisors. Do not cover them with trite advice – 'Live, Love, Laugh', or 'Dream, Relax, Feel'." She says that in her, rather than inspiring the wish to completely change her life, they inspire rage.

There are several rules for mobile phones, for example: "Rule 313: No using speaker phone in public. Ever."

So, I think she is really a serious person. For sport, the first rule is: "Rule 350: No booing." If her book had been handed out at football games, there would have been no problem with fans booing Adam Goodes. She says, save your booing for the baddies in the pantomime, but don't boo elite sportspeople for doing their job well.

488 may seem like a lot of rules, but I appreciate all the work that Kitty put into the making of the book. Mind you, it has provided endless material for her stand-up shows, and some of the rules I remember hearing at her show. She certainly wins the prize for the highest number of rules I have come across. Perhaps it was Stephen Covey who started all this with his *Seven Habits of Highly Effective People* (1990).

Suddenly, marketing people realised that you could sell practically anything if a number was involved. Management books have been particularly rife with numbers: *The Five Dysfunctions of a Team*, *The Five Temptations of a CEO*, *The Four Obsessions of an Extraordinary Executive*. Sometimes, you can even manage to follow it up. Stephen Covey had *The Eighth Habit* (from effectiveness to greatness).

I am not criticising the books themselves. They may be worthwhile. My comment is on this fascination with numbers. Marketers wouldn't use it if it didn't work. The problem is us. It is not just about management books. Fiction is just as rife with numbers: Bryce Courtenay had *The Power of One*.

Kitty Flanagan may take the prize for the most rules of anybody, but I think I have discovered the second place-getter. Hua-Ching Ni is a Chinese teacher and writer who writes about integral medicine, spiritual practice, Chinese philosophy and astrology (no, I haven't read his book about that), T'ai Chi, meditation, and the I Ching. One of his books is *Eight Thousand Years of Chinese Wisdom*. It contains the text of teaching sessions he held with groups of people. You could call them seekers.

In this transcript is a section called "The 180 Observances". So, that is my contender for the second greatest number of rules. What are Hua-Ching Ni's rules like? Are they funny? Well, they don't set out to be, but in different societies, different norms pertain, so some of them might seem funny. The first observance (rule) is: "Do not keep personal servants unless you need help." "Rule 2: Do not sleep with another person's man or woman." "Rule 3: Do not steal people's things." Rule 15 says "Do not set fire to wilderness areas." Rule 16 says "Do not live in opulence."

I think the observances were aimed at people who wanted to come and stay at his retreat. It would not be convenient if they set fire to the bush, and it would not be appropriate if they were anti-social.

Rule 56 says "Do not disrespect any valuable teaching or writing." Rule 158: "Do not be disrespectful of the customs of a new place you are in." And Rule 180: "Do not make your teacher a social figure as an ornament for your ego."

Hua-Ching Ni is not joking, but then, Kitty Flanagan is not always joking. She just has an easy manner, so you are inclined to listen. Her Rule 177 is: "Don't be late." Hua-Ching Ni would say that too. It makes me think it's a fine line between sober and silly. Perhaps she is not a hit among people who hang football jerseys on the wall and boo at football matches.

## 35. Sydney and the Bush

By NSW Education Department, published 1980.

I was so surprised to see *Sydney and the Bush* at the book fair, surprised, because it evoked so many memories. And I had never seen it before at a book fair. It was a hardback in black and white. It was a long time ago, 1980, when it was published. But the book became important to me in 1995, when I was researching for the writing of a book on the centenary of Kyogle Public School.

How did I get the book? In 1980 I was teaching high school, but not at a State school. It was St Mary's in Casino. If I had been working at the State school, it would have been easy to know how I had obtained it. It was a Department of Education production, and it was a pictorial history using their bountiful collection of photographs going back to the early days of the colony. It was the centenary of the *Public Instruction Act 1880*, and I think the book was meant to be something they would be proud of.

Accordingly, they printed many copies, so that anyone who was interested could get one: teachers, ex-pupils, community leaders.... A long list. My memory is that the word came to St Mary's, probably from Casino High School, that there were copies of the book available if we wanted them. I don't remember if we had to pay for them. I think we did, but it was a nominal sum of money. Not many teachers from St Mary's were interested in obtaining a copy, but it was important to me.

Why? I was interested in the history of things. I was interested in the history of schools, where I had ended up working. At Teachers' College we had studied the history of the education system in New South Wales, and I appreciated that it had been a momentous enterprise, because of the number of students, the need to educate pupils in the city as well as the far reaches of the country, and the many obstacles encountered.

Teacher training was an issue that took generations to work out. School accommodation had to start from scratch. The government had to be convinced of the importance of education. There were struggles between the churches and the state about how they would relate to each other in the educational sphere. I remembered names: Peter Board, William Wilkins. I remembered that Henry Parkes was the Premier when the Public Instruction Bill went to Parliament.

I read the book, looked at the photos, then shelved it. There it sat for fifteen years while I was doing other things. In 1988 I wrote a history of the Kyogle Shire, my first book. I thought I did a good job, and it was well-received. I had two children at the primary school in 1994, so I knew that the next year was the year of its centenary, and people were excited about it.

Nevertheless, I was surprised when the school approached me and asked me if I would produce a book for the centenary. They said they thought I had done well with the Shire book, and they trusted me to do well with the school book. I was delighted. I talked to the committee about what they wanted for the book, and they had scattered ideas, but they would leave it up to me.

I could tell what they wanted: they wanted to see themselves in it. At the same time, I wanted it to be more than a smattering of images. When I wrote the Kyogle book, it had a shape, it had context, it had a story. Surely the school had a story too? There were plenty of people who wanted to talk to me, who had a story to tell, and who had photos of their own time at school, and even their parents. But before I got submerged in detail and got lost, I pulled out *Sydney and the Bush*.

My copy looks tattered. I think the silverfish have been eating it, in preference to all the other books they could have been eating.

What I was looking for was context, and themes. When New Park School, the school that became Kyogle Public School, was established in 1895, where did it sit in the State's scheme of things? What was the department trying to achieve through the school? What was the background of the teacher? Where did he live? Who paid for the building? And what themes came and went through the twentieth century?

My copy of the book has markings all the way through, and at some points there are bookmarks inserted. I think I got my money's worth from it. And it made me feel that I could handle this job. I also took a note of the kinds of photos that were included, so that I could look for similar kinds of photos. For example, there was a section in *Sydney and the Bush* about transport to school.

There were photos of buses, of course, but there were also photos of children on horseback: one photo with two children on the one horse, no saddle. One of the Kyogle locals gave me a photo of a horse with seven children on its back. It was an ex-racehorse named Darkie. She told me this photo was real, not posed. Seven children rode this old, sedate horse to school and home each day. To make it more difficult, some children went to the public school and some to St Brigid's, and the horse would stop to drop children off and then continue on its way.

I included some information about the little country schools that were established around Kyogle, mostly one-teacher schools. Upper Horseshoe Creek School, in the valley where I lived, existed from 1932 to 1970. One of the locals pointed out to me the place on the ridge where it had been, about thirty metres above the current road. There was no building anymore, but there was a pine tree that had been planted when the school was there.

I decided to set the book out like a magazine. There would be the main story, which was chronological. I divided it into just four chapters. The book was A4 format, stapled, and 98 pages long. Then there were feature sections, such as travel to school. This theme was so popular with people that there were three parts: horse, bus, and train. One topic was "The getting of the teacher's residence", because that took commitment and effort from the locals, and unless there was a teacher's residence, there could be no school.

There were profiles of people who were still remembered. When the school moved from New Park to town, an Irishman became the headmaster, John Gerald Fagan, and he was held in high esteem. He stayed for over twenty years. Laurice Lyons (nicknamed Tiger) was the headmaster of the school from 1929 to 1933 (the high school was not separate from the primary school until 1954). He also taught history to the high school students. One of his ex-students remembered that he had predicted in 1932 that there would be another great war, after the Japanese had invaded Manchuria, and that the boys in his current class would be soldiers in it. He was right.

I was given poetry, school songs, an eight-year-old's story of travelling to Casino with the school when the young Queen visited in February 1954, and an account from several people and the newspaper about the day the railway line from Kyogle to Brisbane opened, and the whole school went on the train for a day trip to Brisbane. It was 'Tiger' Lyons who organised it, military-style, and he was well-remembered for it.

I had stacks of photos: Christmas events, fancy dress balls, junior farmer days, class groups, sporting representatives. My neighbour in Horseshoe Creek had been the headmaster at the primary school in the late 1970s, so there were photos of him with teachers and pupils too.

It was a tremendously exciting project to work on. When I had finished it, I had the text ready, all typed up on my computer (I had entered the computer age in 1986, sensing that this would be of lifelong importance), ready to hand over to the printer. I had selected the photos I was going to use, and had them ready as well, ready to hand over. I had the photos mapped against the text, so I knew the order, and the place where the photos were going to go.

It was at this point that the printer informed me that he was in dispute with his desktop designer (I think that was the current phrase) and did I think I could do the layout too? I had previously done layout for newsletters on a computer (an Apple IIC), but with my current computer (an Apple IIGS) I didn't have the software to do it. Could I do it? I did! I bought the software and taught myself to use it. I had three weeks to get the job done.

Given that I had decided on a magazine layout, I had to learn a lot of skills. And the quality of my work had to be good enough for the public eye. It took many hours, but I managed to learn the program well enough, and get the job done, and I was happy with the result. I am still happy with what I did.

It was easy to see that a lot of people in the town and the surrounding countryside remembered their school-days with a huge amount of fondness, and my job as the writer and designer was to exhibit that love and honour it. The committee responsible showed that they were deeply grateful for what I had done. I had made a commitment to do the job for free, but at the end the committee made me a payment as an honorarium, which I appreciated.

There was a weekend of celebrations in April 1995. Hundreds of people came back to Kyogle for the weekend. The ABC radio personality Ian McNamara, who hosted the Sunday morning program, *Australia All Over*, came to Kyogle and broadcast the program from the school. He had an additional reason, apart from it being an interesting event. His mother had taught at the school in the late 1930s, as a young, single woman.

She had enjoyed her time at the school, and she wrote a lovely article for the book, recounting clear, happy memories. She even made the statement, "Those years were some of the happiest of my life!"

It is no wonder that I noticed *Sydney and the Bush* at the book fair. It was a reminder of a very satisfying project in my life. I feel that I did in microcosm for Kyogle what that book had done at the level of the whole system of school education in New South Wales over one hundred years.

## 36. Sinning across Spain

By Ailsa Piper, published 2012.

It is an intriguing title. It has the scent of spirited abandonment about it, raunchy and reckless. It has the power of alliteration. One might expect a mischievous read. But the back cover readily confesses that it is the reverse: "I will walk off your sins. 'Pilgrim seeks sinners for mutually beneficial arrangement. Seven Deadlies a speciality.'"

Ailsa Piper proposes to her friends that she will walk a pilgrimage trail across Spain, the *Camino Mozarabe*, that stretches from Granada in the south to Santiago de Compostela in the northwest. She offers to carry a sin for them for the payment of a fee which will support her trip. It is the continuation, or revival, of a medieval tradition where believers paid a pilgrim to 'carry' their sins to holy places and thus buy forgiveness for them. They were called indulgences.

Ailsa will walk for forty days, about 1,200 kilometres in all. She promises to write about the trip as she goes, and send messages back to her supporters along the way. In the end it will become a book. She will carry sins (anger, greed, sloth, pride, lust, envy and gluttony), but not mortal sins (such as violence); behavioural sins she will take, and sins of omission and violations of a moral code.

(I think that the sins of anger, prides etc are classed as mortal sins, and they are contrasted with venial sins, which are of lesser gravity. However, I did not grow up Catholic, so I can't swear to the contemporary use of the terms. And obviously there is a distinction to be made for 'serious' sins that are crimes.)

There are questions. Why do I have a fiction book here? I promised not to diverge into fiction; it's too diverse a field, and probably directionless. I don't remember specifically, but my only explanation is this: a book fair is a crowded and chaotic domain. One is pushed and shoved in many directions. I must have strayed close to the wrong tables and seen the book there.

Or, it may have been wrongly categorised. The sorter may have thought it belonged with Religion, and I did look at that table. Or, the sorter may have put it on the Religion table deliberately, out of mischief. I have seen evidence of their mischief. I saw these two books side by side: *In Praise of Slow*, and *Life in Five Seconds*. Isn't that evidence of humour at work?

However, I may still stand accused of yielding to temptation. Did I stray onto the Fiction tables? I am arguing that there is a chance that I didn't, and I have offered possible explanations. Would a priest then ask me to look deeply into my soul? I still maintain that I kept the faith (on this occasion).

Having explained that, one way or another, I will turn to the question of how I came to have the book in the first place. In September 2017, I went to a Writers' Festival at St Albans. St Albans is a tiny village northwest of Sydney, up past Wisemans Ferry. I had not heard of the festival before, and it looked as if it could be enjoyable. I found some accommodation for the weekend nearby and off I went.

Ailsa Piper was one of the authors. Her session was in an old church. I think that means it was no longer a church, or it might have meant that it was now only used as a church occasionally. I appreciated the organisers' humour, to put *Sinning Across Spain* in a church. She talked about her book, how it came about, what she was thinking at the time, and how she felt about it afterwards. I enjoyed it a lot, and so I bought the book at the festival.

The book could have been a melange of theology that is no longer believable, but it wasn't. If anything, it was a meditation on walking, the simple act of putting one foot in front of the other, often regardless of heavy feelings or physical pain. And it was a foray into the complications and joys of relationships: her encounters on her trip, and her vicarious ruminations on behalf of her friends and their sins.

I discovered that after the book was released (2012), a priest wrote to her, intrigued by her Spanish expedition, and they ended up in an epistolary friendship and, lo and behold, the letters turned into a book, called *The Attachment*. I understand that development. The other book I have that consists of letters is *Reading the Seasons* by Germaine Leece and Sonya Tsakalakis (2021) which I mentioned much earlier. (Having raised this question, I may indeed have other books in the library that consist of letters between two people, but I am not going to pursue that thought at the moment.)

Because the premise of the trip seemed so inescapably medieval and therefore improbable, I was interested to know how Ailsa conceived of the pilgrimage. Here is an example of a sin and how she intended to carry it: "My sin is a desire for vengeance to be visited upon a person. It was so long ago it doesn't even matter anymore, but I still have dreams of them dying in agony and feeling avenged but also guilty." And how would Ailsa carry the sin?

She thought of times when she had also wished for vengeance on someone, and whether she had dealt with that. It prompted her to ask the question of herself more deeply. Sometimes, she felt that she was the one offering forgiveness to the person involved. At times, she was moved enough to cry tears for them.

And she understood implicitly that in offering to carrying a person's sin, she should not commit that same sin when on the walk. For example, she should not tell white lies in order to make a situation easier for herself.

A friend cautioned her as she was about to leave that she was tempting evil into her life by taking on the sins of others. She should

166

be wary, because sin and guilt are potent. There are forces around us that we don't understand, and they could "hijack her beautiful intention". Ailsa considered the warning, but decided that she was here to live, not just to take up space.

She was nervous. She met two men (a gay couple) on the plane from Rome to Barcelona. When they found out about her plans, they expressed concern that she was doing it alone. They insisted that she take their phone numbers, and call them immediately if anything went wrong. One of them gave her a card, a holy picture of a saint, the *Santo Nino de Alocha*. He said it was the patron saint of pilgrims.

The journey was said to be in three acts, like a play. Act One was for the body; the pilgrim is taught lessons by their body. Act Two was for the mind; one has to battle with the relentlessness of the journey. And Act Three is for the spirit; pilgrims reap the rewards of the struggles they have had with the body and the mind. Perhaps they will get to understand something of the Thinker behind the thoughts.

One pilgrimage patron confessed to envy about Ailsa. She said that Ailsa always appeared to live a life free of fear, sadness or doubt. Ailsa thought: "To me, awash in fear, it seemed as if the words were written about another person." But she wrote, "The confession irritated me"! One is ever faced with one's own sins.

On beginning the walk, she is assailed by the thought of those who have no home. She is not one of them; she can always go home. She gets an email from a friend back home, who gives her the quote: "Whenever we are truly present, wherever we are, we bring peace." It seems pertinent.

And, too, she quotes a line from Rainer Maria Rilke: "So we are grasped by what we cannot grasp."

She comes across people in the countryside, farmers at work in their fields, who ask her what she is doing. She says the words, in the little Spanish she knows: "*Camino. Peregrina.*" Pilgrim. They say "*Vaya con Dios."* Go with God. In a sense, her journey is for them too. A group of orchard workers name her "lady kangaroo" and say she has *'duende'* – natural force. Others offer her gifts and ask her to say prayers for them.

Occasionally she came across another pilgrim and would walk with them for a while, although she said she preferred walking alone. One companion was 'Herr T', a German theologian. They had a disagreement about whether people could be born evil and therefore be beyond redemption. Ailsa held that evil generally was the end result of the circumstances of a person's life, and could be remedied. Herr T did not agree. "In my country, we have had to look into the darkness of the human heart. Evil exists."

Ailsa held her ground. Herr T alluded to Cain and Abel in the book of Genesis. Why were they different? He said the learning that must occur is at the level of humanity as a whole. We must learn to recognise evil and be strong enough to face it down. It was an unresolved conversation. Two people of good will, and with something important at stake. The road conspired to let the question sit, as she seesawed between aloneness and incidents where strangers were kind to her.

When she periodically accessed email messages, people at home were pursuing their thoughts about sin: inability to accept the past, fear of living without white lies, guilt at sins of omission. They asked for answers which she didn't have. She was merely a pilgrim.

In the small city of Cordoba, there was news of a volcano eruption in Iceland. The ash from it had stopped plane flights all around Europe.

She meets Herr T again and they continue to argue theology. They discuss how we know what God thinks. She goes to Mass, and mingles with old people who attend Mass faithfully. She admires their faith. Later, she discovers that Herr T had been at the Mass as well, and it precipitated a crisis of faith for him. Was he losing his faith? He was scared.

One of her correspondents asks her if she is committing the sin of simony: asking another to do your penance for you. She considers that, but concludes that it is a question of her intention, and her intention is pure. She is a pilgrim: faith in motion. She just keeps turning up.

She keeps seeing herself as sinful. In an episode of fearful, flooding rain, "every squelching step was punishment for my selfishness, my gluttony for solitude, my impatience towards an older person (Herr T)." Thankfully, she is aware that masochism, too, is undesirable. After this, Herr T disappears from the story.

She goes to Mass in another pueblo (small village) and finds herself longing for the simple certainty of faith she felt as a young girl. And, after rain, there are days of sunshine when walking is magnificent and she is unable to keep her focus on sin, and she feels guilty for that. She endures more vicissitudes, tears and anger, and books into a musty room with fleas because she was not paying attention.

Another companion is amused at her carrying the sins of others. He says she should be making some sins of her own! She thinks that a life lived among Catholic ritual, with the year punctuated by saints' days, is hard to release.

Ailsa has divided the *camino* into three stages, three acts. After the city of Merida she is in Act Two. It seems that she is easier about walking in company, not so determined to be alone. Perhaps she is learning tolerance. But there is still a tension, for she is on a mission; this is not a holiday. She was answerable to her sinners and herself, and solitude was essential.

What did she think about when she was walking? Nothing, she says. I do not think, but I am conscious. And in company, there was always the delicacy of speaking and hearing across languages: Spanish, English, German, French, and wrestling with the potential for misunderstanding. All the while knowing that the *camino* is not as hard as being at home; home is the real life. And seeing that as the wisdom that comes of walking for twelve hundred kilometres.

"Traveller, there is no road, the road is made by walking." She is becoming detached from the sins she is carrying. Whose sins are they? She was becoming increasingly aware that she herself was capable of all those sins. In Zamora she reads a sign: "The value of the *camino* is in the love you offer by walking." So, she thinks, that is what you can do.

And as well as giving, one also receives: "Never have I been so much myself as in the journeys I have taken alone and on foot", that being a quote from Jean-Jacques Rousseau. One of her correspondents asks her, that if there can be payment made to erase sin, can there also be payments relating to the accumulation of virtue? But Ailsa is far from answering that question.

On the pilgrim's way, in the middle of a deluge, carrying her heavy pack, she has a breakdown, sobbing, falling to her knees. Grief erupted in her, a mysterious onslaught. She remembered the previous *camino* she had been on, and being in the cathedral at the end of it, not feeling the rush of validation she thought she would feel.

Now she saw that the scene in the cathedral was external; the catechism was external. What was real was internal, and more uncertain. What had she left on the roadside, but that desire for external certainty? In its stead was the acceptance of herself: "My faith may not fit in cathedrals, but it is no less meaningful for that."

After that episode, things did not become easier. The thought dogged her that all this travail was empty of meaning. Meaning was just the crunch of boots on gravel. She writes, as one does, to lure meaning to the surface: "A saint is a tree beside the road. A sermon is a story told at sunset. Divinity is the moment when heartbeats and footsteps align, find each other and mark miles together. A miracle is the gift of homemade food from a woman who is a stranger to a pilgrim on the road."

And "*Buen camino*" is a blessing. Good road.

The words of Rilke say, "Let everything happen to you – beauty and terror. Just keep going. No feeling is final. Don't let yourself lose me."

She makes it to Santiago de Compostela, where she went to Mass and received her certificate (the *compostelas*) from the church to say she had completed the *camino*. But she is compelled to go a further one hundred kilometres to the ocean, Cape Finisterre, the end of the world: the final destination for pilgrims. She burned the list of sins on the beach.

At the end of the *camino*, she feels that she has learned to travel peacefully, and to travel in company. What does she know? That life has sun and shadow. That life is story, and the more truthful we are in our stories, the more freedom we gain. And that we are all connected, and we owe it to ourselves to acknowledge that fact in our actions and our words. And we do not know what happens when we die, but this life is enough.

At the end, she says, there is gratitude and the present. And the people who made their commitment to her pilgrimage, the sinners, reported that it had prompted them to make changes in their lives. As she walked, they had pondered.


In the end, you have to integrate all of it. And in the stories there are many thoughts, beyond "He said and she said" and "This happened and that happened". So, Ailsa Piper leaves the question of how I categorise her book. The beauty of having my own library is that I choose, and whatever I choose is correct. It is my decision. I have become attracted to the idea of having a "Recently Acquired" shelf. I have a nominal twelve-month limit on this shelf.

That rule has enabled me to defer a more permanent decision, but *Sinning Across Spain* has exceeded that limit now. However, this current project has necessitated a shelf of its own, the "Current Project" shelf, and therefore, the book can live here a while longer. Where then?

I have created a 'Biography' category, because, although I fought the idea of it, it does help sometimes. It is a testament to the idea from *Hamlet*: "There are more things in heaven and earth, Horatio, than are dreamt of in your philosophy." But I consider it to be a category of last resort. I could put *Sinning Across Spain* there.

However, I search hard for a better alternative. For example, Elizabeth Gilbert's book, *The Signature of All Things*, went in the category, "Books about the Big Story of Humankind". Where could *Sinning Across Spain* go? It could go in "Soul-Searching", or even "Losing My Religion". If I had a category for "Walking" it would go there. It could go in "Christian Books". It deserves to go there, because it is so focused on sin.

What did she realise at the end? That there is gratitude and the present. Life is not circumscribed by, or defined by, sin. It is in the nature of life to mature and expand, and we ride that dragon. On the way, we learn to rein in our ego, and to be kind. When the sun is swallowed by the earth, we should direct our attention to our own inner light. The fulfilment we seek is within us.

These are mere words. Meaning is the crunch of boots on gravel.

## 37. Eats, Shoots and Leaves
By Lynne Truss, published 2003.

Book fairs are exhausting mentally. Your head is spinning around between hundreds of different subjects and thousands of different perspectives on these subjects. Your brain is hovering, thinking about if and when to intervene and say, "You should buy that book!" At the same time, it is competing with the voice that says "No more books! You have more than enough! You will never get to read any extra!"

But my sphere of interests is expanding. There are more reasons to say "Yes, you should get that book. It will give you more perspective on that topic. It will answer that question you have always been asking."

And language, well, language is the beginning of it all. I think back to primary school lessons about words and grammar rules, and how absorbed I was. Now I can at least understand how bored some of the other children were. But I was doing my apprenticeship in words. I was learning. Lynne Truss described a similar experience of childhood in the United Kingdom, oblivious that other children were not interested at all.

I noted with satisfaction that Kitty Flanagan's book, *488 Rules for Life*, has a chapter on Language. It is Chapter Four of her fifteen chapters. Of course, her rules are funny, although I am also sure that most people would find one or two of her rules to be disquieting, because they are guilty of breaking them, or have colleagues who do so. Rule 79: Don't describe inanimate objects as 'sexy'. Rule 78: Avoid using adjectives such as 'delicious' or 'yummy' in non-food contexts. Rule 83: Don't refer to your 'tribe'.

However, I noted with a droll smile that *Eats, Shoots and Leaves* was classed as "Reference / Humour". The categorisation was included with the barcode on the back cover of the book.

My first copy of the book? Someone gave it to me at Christmas when I worked at the publishing company. An appropriate gift. The book is a winner straightaway, because the title comes with a funny story. A panda walks into a café. He orders a sandwich, eats it, then draws a gun and fires two shots into the air. (In some versions of this story, the panda walks into a bar.)

The waiter says, "Why did you do that?' And the panda says, "Just following the manual."

"What manual is that?" asks the waiter. The panda pulls out a manual on animals, and the waiter looks up 'Panda'. It says, "Bear-like mammal, native to China. Eats, shoots and leaves." The problem is the poor punctuation: the stray comma. Lesson One in "Punctuation is important".

Another story I heard, much more succinct, was a child exclaiming, "Let's eat grandma!" In that case, the insertion of a comma would have allayed grandma's fears.

I had to think about writing "Lynne Truss's book". I sense two schools of thought on this. Perhaps it should be Lynne Truss' book". Does she clarify? Indeed, she does. Because of her own name, she had encountered the problem. Her preference is for "Truss's book". She also opts for Keats's poems". But she accepts that some people were brought up differently, and they are insistent (adamant!) that it should be "Keats' poems".

In some matters, she says, it is not a matter of absolute rights and wrongs. It may be a question of how it sounds. For example, in a discussion of the tennis player, Jimmy Connors, a writer referred to "Connors's forehand". But Truss says there are exceptions. If the name ends with an 's' sound, there should be no extra 's'. Accordingly, it is Moses' tablets and Jesus' disciples. These examples make Connors's forehand hard to understand. As Kitty Flanagan observes, it is difficult to be right.

Years ago I heard (only by chance) that geographical names, at least in New South Wales, had dropped all apostrophes. It was a ruling by the Geographical Names Board. So, Thompson's Corner is now Thompsons Corner, and Wiseman's Ferry is Wisemans Ferry. However, as Truss notes, in England, an institution can choose to retain an apostrophe in its name, for example, St Thomas' Hospital. That is its prerogative.

Beyond such arguments, there are questions of right, wrong and ambiguity. I agree with Truss: without punctuation there is no reliable way of communicating meaning. The comma saves grandma from being eaten. For all that one has a story or message to tell, words and punctuation are the bridge that one has to cross.

She cites many metaphors for punctuation. It is the stitching that holds the fabric of language in shape. Punctuation marks are the traffic signals of language: they tell us when to slow down or detour. Or more delicately: punctuation is a courtesy designed to help readers to understand a story without stumbling. Or, punctuation herds the words together, and keeps others apart.

To emphasise the role of punctuation, she gives two versions of the same set of words: (1) A woman, without her man, is nothing; (2) A woman: without her, man is nothing. Punctuation can make meanings opposite.

You could say that punctuation is two-thirds by rule and one-third by current convention and personal taste. The aim is clarity. Truss cites the movie *Two Weeks Notice*. It was advertised without an apostrophe at the end of 'Weeks'. This is not a matter of taste; it is simply wrong. The correct version is *Two Weeks' Notice*.

It is customary for older people (like me) to rail against the education that occurred in schools after the 1960s. It was a time dominated by the idea that teaching grammar was unnecessary, and indeed, it would get in the way of children's creativity. Truss has this view of schooling in the United Kingdom. I have that view of schooling in Australia.

Truss notes that this is not to say there was ever a golden age of grammar. The *Oxford Companion to English Literature* holds, with respect to the apostrophe: "There never was a golden age in which the rules for the possessive apostrophe were clear-cut and known, understood and followed by most educated people." That is a sobering thought. It is not saying "most people" but "most educated people"!

Accomplished English expression requires a grasp of a great manner of punctuation marks. Commas are of critical importance, but fashion has pushed them around. Truss notes the wars that have been fought in editorial circles. I call them the STET wars. You write an article, and then it goes to the sub-editor. They have been schooled in the philosophy that commas just get in the way of the flow, and they take most of them out and send it back to you.

You read it again for sense, and discover that ambiguity and confusion of meaning are now rampant, so you mark it up and send it back to them to finalise. Against every comma that you wish to retain you write 'STET', meaning "let it stand". In her case, said Truss, sometimes there were STETs written all the way down the margins of the pages.

My own experience at the publishing company was similar. There were particular sub-editors who seemed to be on a mission to eradicate commas, and I was savage in my response: STET, STET, STET! What made it worse was that some of the material I was writing was on employment law, and an absent or misplaced comma could be perilous. I read one news story about a large company in the US that ended up having to pay $150,000 to its employees because a court deemed that it had misinterpreted its employment agreement: all to do with the difference a comma made in a sentence about payment for overtime.

Respect for the comma!

Respect also for the hyphen. An "oft told tale" reads more appropriately as an "oft-told tale". 'Oft' and 'told' are bound together here. Separating them gives rise to ambiguity (and perhaps also, discomfort). There are two possible sins: the hyphen can be under utilised (which should be under-utilised); or the two words can be pushed together inappropriately, as in "slowmoving traffic". And yet there is a whole world of change underway (not under way). "Second hand" and "second-hand" have become accepted as "secondhand". But "re-enter" has not become "reenter".

Truss notes that in the early twentieth century, instead of writing "Oxford Street", one wrote "Oxford-street". I can confirm that I have seen this usage in Australian newspapers in the 1930s (Castlereagh-street), when I have been pursuing family history. So, change is ever upon us, and usage must adapt. Yet, the communication of meaning is still imperative.

Truss thinks it is unfortunate that a period of under-education in grammar has coincided with the advent of the internet, and the concomitant explosion of global self-publishing. She asserts that it is a shame punctuation has been thrown out as worthless by people who have no knowledge of it, and no idea of the problems this is causing.

We are subject to the exigencies of the internet world; for example, web pages and emails have very often led us to dispense with spaces between words. But one must wrestle with ambiguity. It was once suggested to me that I should have a website called "writerinaction" and I decided not to do that. Why? Because, does it mean "writer in action" or "writer inaction"? "In action" sounds great, but "inaction" is not so attractive.

Truss was writing not long after the start of the internet age (2003). Yet there is still the reality of ambiguity and the need for meaning to be clear. At the end of her book she remains committed to the cause of punctuation. I think, if you have something to say, that's half the problem solved. The remaining half is to express it clearly, and you cannot take that for granted., even if, or especially if, people around you are writing sloppily.

### 38. I Never Metaphor I Didn't Like
By Mardy Grothe, published 2008.

If Lynne Truss's book cautions us to show care when we write, to safeguard our meaning, Mardy Grothe's book shows us the flowery effusions that language makes possible or, you might say, that language is prone to. If Truss's book starts with a joke: "A panda walks into a bar…", then so does Grothe's: "I never metaphor I didn't like". Although, one might ask, what is a 'phor'?

I bought the book originally at a book fair, simply because I thought the book might be amusing. Although I generally avoid the Humour section at book fairs (there is a long list of categories that I don't need to peruse), I am not completely averse to humour. And of course, the book was never going to be all just frivolity.

Early on he quotes Kahlil Gibran (who turns up everywhere): "One may not reach the dawn save by the path of the night." And, he echoes a thought that occurred to Ailsa Piper: "Do not go where the path may lead; go instead where there is no path and leave a trail" (Ralph Waldo Emerson). And the source of M. Scott Peck's title is disclosed: "Two roads diverged in a wood and I…. I took the one less travelled by, and that has made all the difference" (Robert Frost).

Ailsa Piper learned the association of sun with shadow. Grothe tells us that Albert Camus said, "There is no sun without shadow, and it is essential to know the night." Grothe says that he has been an avid collector of quotations for decades, and it has been helpful to him: "I was in the depths of a dark winter [metaphorically]. Now, however, I was beginning to break through to a deeper level of understanding about myself and what I needed to do with my life." He puts this down to his "investment in a reflective reading program".

He draws on Franz Kafka for a metaphor about the value of reading: "A book should serve as an ice-axe to break the frozen sea within us." It is a powerful metaphor. Kafka went on to say that a book should waken us like a fist hammering on our skull! Grothe follows up with Rudyard Kipling: "Words are, of course, the most powerful drug used by mankind."

The beauty of books is the words and ideas they contain. Grothe rightly asserts that the most powerful words are those that contain pictures. As the front cover of his book attests, quoting Robert Frost: "An idea is a feat of association, and the height of it is a good metaphor." Two ideas are hauled together, one to illustrate the other, often in surprising and remarkable - and memorable - ways.

"If you board the wrong train, it is no use running along the corridor in the other direction" (Dietrich Bonhoeffer). That is an unforgettable image, and it forces you to think deeply about the implications of the association. This is different from direct instruction, which says, "Do this; don't do that." It urges you to search your own mind, thinking up ideas about how this could be applicable to you.

I am always wary of statements being glib or trite. These are easy traps to fall into. Gustave Flaubert even compiled a book of such sayings: *A Dictionary of Platitudes* (1913). The appropriate warning comes from Frederic Chopin: "Every difficulty slurred over will be a ghost to disturb your repose later on." And "Acting without thinking is like shooting without aiming" (B.C. Forbes).

Sometimes, however, there may be truth in a saying that is best served to oneself rather than inflicting it on others: "We must embrace pain and burn it as fuel for our journey." Later he quotes Florynce Kennedy: "Trying to help an oppressed person is like trying to put your arm around somebody with a sunburn."

Even books attract a caution: "But beware you be not swallowed up in books! An ounce of love is worth a pound of knowledge" (John Wesley).

And Lin Yutang (*The Importance of Living*) is cited: "However vague they are, dreams have a way of concealing themselves and leave us no peace until they are translated into reality."

Sometimes the visual image that a metaphor calls up can be enough to shock us: "Vocations which we wanted to pursue, and didn't, bleed, like colours, on the whole of our existence" (Honore de Balzac).

After this submersion in the human condition, Grothe comes to humour, "the shock absorber of life". He quotes Mary Hirsch: "Humour is a rubber sword: it allows you to make a point without drawing blood." Reading this chapter, my observation is that humour tends to be local, constrained by both time and place (some of the sayings go back more than twenty years, and Grothe is American). Some things translate well enough: "He looked at me as if I were a side dish he hadn't ordered" (Ring Lardner).

Other jokes and metaphors get lost. But then, Grothe could quote E.B. White to me: "Analysing humour is like dissecting a frog. Few people are interested and the frog dies of it."

This is followed by a chapter of insults, not necessary to perpetuate, except for an acknowledgment of Winston Churchill insulting another politician: "He occasionally stumbled over the truth, but hastily picked himself up and hurried on as if nothing had happened."

There is an exquisite chapter called "Definitive Metaphors" (in Grothe's judgement), starting with a definition of 'Definition': "A definition is the enclosing a wilderness of idea within a wall of words" (Samuel Butler). Another sample is a definition of fame: "Fame is a fickle food upon a shifting plate" (Emily Dickinson). And, unsolicited advice: "the junk mail of life" (Bern Williams).

"Gratitude is the heart's memory" (French proverb).

"Life is the art of drawing without an eraser" (John W. Gardner). This is the title of a chapter. It is the chapter that is most in danger of being glib or trite. Summing up life in a single sentence is fraught with danger, but it is what words entice us to do. "Life is painting a picture, not doing a sum" (Oliver Wendell Holmes). Yes, there is wisdom there.

What about this? "Life is a journey, but don't worry, you'll find a parking spot at the end" (Isaac Asimov). What does that mean, anything at all? Or, "Life is a moderately good play with a badly written third act" (Truman Capote). I suppose these are just two ways of saying that it's disappointing that we die.

"Life is like a cobweb, not an organisation chart" (H. Ross Perot). Or William Shakespeare: "The web of our life is of a mingled yarn, good and ill together". One can get lost in all these metaphors. I find it is best if one takes small doses. Many of the metaphors Grothe presents are assertions that life is fundamentally good, or similarly strong assertions that life is bad. But his last saying is: "Life is a rainbow which also includes black" (Yegeny Yevtushenko).

The last thing Grothe talks about is writing, just as the last books from Knox Grammar that I talk about are on words and books. He gives many metaphors for writing. From F. Scott Fitzgerald: "All good writing is swimming under water and holding your breath." On reading novels, he quotes Saul Bellow: "With a novelist, like a surgeon, you have to get a feeling that you've fallen into good hands – someone from whom you can accept the anaesthetic with confidence."

Another perspective on novels is from Albert Camus: "A novel is never anything but a philosophy put into images." Similarly, Virginia Woolf said, "Fiction is like a spider's web, attached ever so lightly perhaps, but still attached to life at all four corners."

The categorisation 'Novel' may be problematic. Take, for example, *Sinning across Spain*, which may or may not have been in the Fiction section at the book fair. Is it a novel? Obviously not; it is a first-person account of a trip. The only fictionalisation, we assume, is in the naming of the people she meets on the journey, one of whom never even gets a name; he is simply "the amigo". In the testimonies at the front of the book, *The Examiner* calls it "good travel writing". *Good Reading* says, "This account is filled with landscape, history, philosophy, friendships, hospitality, poetic self-expression and *albuerges* (pilgrim inns)."

There must be a point at which people start using the word 'novel' to describe a book, leaving out a great many books, some of which are travel writing, some of which are biography, current affairs, or another (non-fictional) topic. *The Signature of All Things* (Elizabeth Gilbert) is a novel. *The Guardian* called it 'historical-fantastical', but also said it was "packed with authenticating detail".

I stand by the category I use: "Reflections on Experience". It admits the truth of the stories told, and the journeys into philosophy, and avoids the squirmish label 'Memoir'. I would admit Ailsa Piper's book if it needed a home, but she is probably quite amused with "good travel writing".

Talking about writing more generally, Edna Ferber said, "Only amateurs say that they write for their own amusement. Writing is not an amusing occupation. It is a combination of ditch-digging, mountain-climbing, treadmill, and childbirth. Writing may be interesting, absorbing, exhilarating, racking, relieving, but amusing? Never!"

## 6   Visiting a Book Fair (Again) – Castle Hill

I visited the Castle Hill book fair run by Lifeline on Sunday 8 October. It was in the hall of Oakhill College, a private school. Did I buy books? Well, yes. But not many, and most of them were small books. Did I see any books that I already own? Last time, at Knox Grammar, I found nineteen books that were already in my library. This time, in contrast, I found none. None; not one.

You could think of various reasons for this, I suppose. The locality was different. Probably the source of the books was different, although I don't know how these factors would make a difference. And maybe I didn't look carefully enough. Maybe I wasn't tuned in enough to remember what books I had in my library. Or perhaps, statistically, this is an insignificant event. Variations are bound to happen.

I was just looking. I was prepared to walk out empty-handed. In the end, I bought ten books. But if you look at that in terms of the total stacked height, it was only 150 mm. What was the range of subject matter? There were a few directions.

One area was, loosely, history. I have to be more specific than that, don't I? Yes. One book was a history of Tasmania (*A Short History of Tasmania*, Lloyd Robson). Given that I have been focused, lately, on my great great grandparents, Sarah Crosby and Edward Lewis, and their experiences as convicts in Tasmania, this purchase is easily understandable. I went to Tasmania in August 2023, and when I came home I produced a book from the diary I kept while travelling: *Travel with a Pen*.

I also bought *The Scots in Australia*, which is relevant to my study of the Mackie family, my mother's mother's family. And one other person, Ellen Welch, who came to Australia alone in 1841 from Fife in Scotland, in company with many other single women who were venturing to the colony to find their future, and most likely, their husband. Ellen married William Archer, a convict. They are also my great great grandparents.

Another history book I bought was *Martin of Martin Place*, written by Elena Grainger (born 1909). She wrote poetry as well as a series of books and articles on aspects of Australian history. I have always been curious about Sir James Martin because one wonders whether one is related. I am not; he came from Cork in Ireland. My Martin relatives come from Cornwall. But I have started reading the book, and I am finding him to be an admirable and interesting character.

Another loosely historical book I bought was *Antique Maps*, that was a bound version of a series of postcards of maps in the Library of Congress. There were some lovely maps in it, but little sign of

Australia. The only trace I saw was in a 1660 world map, where Australia was shown at the fringe, with the western and northern coastlines filled in, but nothing else.

We have the Dutch to thank for what was there. Dirk Hartog, Abel Tasman and William Dampier had charted that during the seventeenth century, although not because they were looking for it. Sailors had learned that, to get to east Asian destinations such as Java, the best way was to follow the winds of the fortieth parallel (the Roaring Forties) east, then to turn north at a suitable point. The difficulty was that the determination of longitude was at that time mostly a matter of guesswork, because neither accurate instruments nor methods had yet been devised.

When I went looking in my library for a book about this business (Frank Welsh's *Great Southern Land*, published by Penguin in 2005), I found another book: *Martin of Martin Place*. Oh. Okay, so I did buy a book that I already owned. This means I didn't realise that I already owned it, and it means I shouldn't have bought it. And I shouldn't have been so adamant about not seeing a single book that I owned. "One should beware of being too adamant." In Kitty Flanagan's book it would be Rule 489.

However, I can justify my purchase of the book. The spine of the dust cover on the one I own is terribly faded, almost white and unreadable, while the new copy's dust cover is like new, so I would have wanted to purchase it anyway (for four dollars).

That's it for history. What else did I buy? I found some older books, 'older' meaning before about 1980. (*Martin of Martin Place* was one of them. It was published in 1970.) I bought a tiny novel by Graham Greene, *The Quiet American*. I had heard of this book but I know nothing about it. Time to find out. It is just over two hundred pages, but in small format (4 ½ by 6 ½ inches; 11 mm by 17 mm). It was first published in 1955. My version is a Penguin Twentieth Century Classic, 1973.

The back cover says "*The Quiet American* is a terrifying portrait of innocence at large. While the French Army in Indo-China is grappling with Vietminh, back at Saigon a young and high-minded American begins to channel economic aid to a Third Force." I probably should have read it in 1970 when I was turning twenty and was eligible for conscription for the Vietnam War. (I spoke about that in *Long Time Approaching*, my "incomplete memoir".)

I bought a hard cover book that was published (in Melbourne) in 1939: *The Bond of Poetry*. It was edited by J.J. Stable. It is sub-titled "A book of verse for Australian schools". Why? I am thinking over my life, and one path could have been as an English teacher. Mind you, this idea had already faded by the time I left high school. I have no regrets. However, I have a lingering curiosity about what was taught at school, what was thought to be important, how this has changed, and what were the reasons why some things were discarded and others retained.

The book is set out in three parts: Narrative, Descriptive and Patriotic. I was always a bit shy about patriotism. Often, it brings out the worst in people. I suppose there is a good way of being proud, but it is a delicate balance. Mostly, it is a version of tribalism: Us versus Them. The true venture is to find how we are all one, and to strive for that: the only worthwhile realism.

Having said that, some of the poems in this section are about Australia as a place rather than Australia as a polity. The first poem is the classic "My country" by Dorothy Mackellar. It is a great paeon of praise and love for a land that is not always gentle: "I love a sunburnt country, a land of sweeping plains, of ragged mountain ranges, of droughts and flooding rains. I love her far horizons, I love her jewel sea, her beauty and her terror – the wide brown land for me!" She wrote this in 1904, at the age of nineteen, and I would say it has become the lens through which many people began to appreciate the harsh wonder that Australia can be, and to accept it as home.

This section includes much about England. I remember, this book was published on the verge of World War Two, when Australians mostly felt vulnerable and distant from the centre of the Empire. Even Henry Lawson has a poem called "England yet". He said (in 1917), "We learn our England, and in peace forget, to learn in storm she is England yet." Perhaps he would not have felt the same during World War Two, when Australia stood by itself, and then forged a bond with the United Sates.

The first poem in the Narrative section is "The sliprails and the spur" by Henry Lawson, and the second is "The man from Snowy River" by Andrew Barton (Banjo) Paterson. The first poem is about love and distance in outback Australia; the second is that great, poetic saga that was made into a grand movie. I think this is not bad as a young person's introduction to the world of musical language in the context of Australia.

This section also includes the whole of "The rime of the ancient mariner" by Samuel Taylor Coleridge. Today it would be considered somewhat remote from Australian concerns. Yet, the concerns of poetry are not merely patriotic. It is meant to be a doorway to a larger world of personal meaning. It is, I suppose, more a question of what is deemed to be relevant in the contemporary world.

Enough of poetry! And yet, I saw another hardcover book (a thin one) and was curious. The cover was plain, with the title in small capital letters: *NYMPHS OF THE VALLEY.* This meant nothing to me, but the author's name did: KAHLIL GIBRAN. I had spent some years as a young man absorbing his poetry and philosophy, and I have several of his books. *The Prophet* has become a classic book. He offered a heartfelt insight into spirituality, regardless of the trials of the world. He offered a vision of the noble soul.

I had not heard of *Nymphs of the Valley,* so I was delighted. (It turned out to be short stories, not poems.) I will add this book to my collection. It was published in Melbourne in 1948 by William Heinemann. Books still had sombre covers then. It is a slim volume, just fifty-five pages. It was translated from the Arabic by H.M. Nahmad. It gives a list of his books. *The Prophet* was published in 1923. A testimony from Claude Bragdon says, "His power came from some great reservoir of spiritual life else it could not have been so universal and so potent, but the majesty and beauty of the language with which he clothed it were all his own."

Of course, I got curious about who Claude Bragdon is. He is in Wikipedia, and he offers a glimpse into yet another world. He was an American architect, and a significant one. He designed Rochester's New York Central Railroad Station. He was allied with the American arts and craft movement of the early 1900s, with people such as Gustav Stickley (I mention the latter in my book, *Travel with a Pen*).

I assume Bragdon made the comment on Kahlil Gibran because he too had a spiritual perspective. The article in Wikipedia says he worked in the progressive tradition associated with Frank Lloyd Wright, although he distinguished himself from the individualism which was characteristic of the latter's work. Bragdon argued that "only an 'organic architecture' based on nature could foster a democratic community in an industrial capitalist society."

The book consists of three short stories, which I have not yet read. The stories are told in simple language. 'Martha', the first story, starts this way:

"Her father died while she was still in the cradle, and her mother before she was ten years old. She was left an orphan in the house of a poor neighbour who lived with his wife and children and existed on the fruits of the soil in a small isolated hamlet amidst the beautiful valleys of Lebanon."

The only oddity in the book is that there are said to be four illustrations by the author included (facing pages 16, 26, 36, and 50), but there is only one. Nothing seems to have been removed from the book. There are always more questions than answers.

The next book I bought was a flamboyant affair, and another book I had never heard of, although I had certainly heard of the author: Oscar Wilde. The title? *Lord Arthur Savile's Crime*. It was in hardback, but jauntily rendered, with a scrawled sketch of a gentleman's head with a top hat on the front cover. One assumes this is Lord Arthur. Oscar Wilde's signature is below the title, in lieu of his typed name.

You can read the book at Gutenberg.org. It was first published in 1891 (according to Fluck, see below; according to Gutenberg, it was first published in 1887) and then enjoyed numerous editions. Apparently, Oscar Wilde kept refining the story as the years went by. When was my edition published? I do not know; there is a reference to 1946 in Fluck's afterword, so it must have been around that date. It was published by Joseph Henry, Melbourne, but before the time when giving the year of publication was the norm. About Joseph Henry the Melbourne publisher I have been able to find out nothing.

The book has numerous wood engravings by Dorothea Braby. There are six of these. They are full-page, stylistic, cartoonish, and in black and one other colour (eg red, yellow, green). Already you get the idea that Wilde writes about people's pretensions and vanities.

I haven't read the book yet, but I can tell you this: at the back of the book is a section called "About the book". The writer of this section, Edward J. Fluck, says that Wilde would have been delighted with this edition, because he thought a book should be a thing of pleasure. (Edward J. Fluck translated Flaubert's book, *A Dictionary of Platitudes*.) It seems that Wilde was satirised before he had even published a line, in the Gilbert and Sullivan opera, *Patience*. He was depicted as a "prater of plausible paradoxes and quipster of crisp epigrams", and an apostle of the "art for art's sake" movement.

Wilde responded with the quip: "Caricature is the tribute mediocrity pays to genius." Wilde is famous for many plays, such as *The Picture of Dorian Gray*, *Lady Windemere's Fan*, and *The Importance of Being Ernest*. Apparently, Wilde most enjoyed relating his stories to friends whilst strolling, and writing them down was somewhat of a chore. Accordingly, the stories continued to evolve.

Fluck says Sir Henry Irving heard Lord Arthur's ingenious adventure outlined in five minutes this way, and he jotted it down from memory. Some people also said they preferred Wilde's spoken version more than the written version. Wilde used these short stories as proving grounds for his epigrams, which he polished and transferred to his plays. So, I have this story to look forward to.

Another book I bought was a small hardback book by Michael Leunig, the Australian cartoonist: *The Curly Pyjama Letters*. (In fact, six of the ten books I bought were hardbacks. This was not by design; I have no argument against paperbacks.) I have numerous Leunig books in my library. Leunig is good for the soul.

The book contains twenty-nine letters exchanged between the lone voyager Vasco Pyjama and his friend and mentor Mr Curly of Curly Flat. They purport to be but a small fragment of a vast correspondence between them. Few details are known of their lives. The rumours and snippets "elude substantiation". I could quote from the book, but it is best just to imbibe it whole, to rest in its mellow but insightful ambience.

A while ago, there was a fuss about people who were "living treasures" of Australia. Such efforts are doomed to failure, because it puts a person on a throne, and infers that they are beyond criticism. Ironically, some people then want to knock them down off that throne, so they find fault with them. It just leads to arguments. But if I had a list of living treasures, there are some people who would be on my list. Say, people whose literary work is good for the soul.

Lastly, I bought (another hardback book,) *The Book of Courtly Love*, by Andrea Hopkins. It was published in 1994 by Aquarian Books (an imprint of Harper Collins, London). There are many aspects of this life to think about, and over time, to reconsider. Romantic love is one of them. I find myself adopting a social-class perspective when reading such books.

The idea of courtly love may have been salient to those who had the time and leisure to entertain it, but for the peasant classes, it was merely a fantasy. One loved and married within the realm of practicality. One did not allow oneself to wander, or did not have the luxury of doing so.

Nevertheless, Hopkins' argument is that the wealthier classes are where ideas are germinated, and from there they flow down into all society. It is like Miranda Priestley's (Meryl Streep) argument about fashion in the movie, *The Devil Wears Prada*. You may not be interested in fashion, or even aware of it, but it plays out at a high level in society, then trickles down to ordinary girls. Just so, ordinary people are influenced by romantic ideas about love, not just in Medieval times, but today. The romantic theme in books and movies is evidence enough.

I wrote about love and marriage in my book, *Long Time Approaching*, drawing on the book, *Committed*, by Elizabeth Gilbert, and the I Ching writer, Hua-Ching Ni. Distinctions have to be made between love and marriage and the responsibilities that families bring. Hopkins doesn't rule that we are helpless in the face of romantic love, or that we should trample it out of existence. She raises the questions for consideration. She talks about people giving all for love, and even dying for love, but also, in Andreas Capellanius' "Rules of Love", notes that "It is well-known that love is always either growing or declining". And yet she also says that Capellanius' Rules of Love may be an elaborate intellectual joke for his audience in the late twelfth century.

She ends by asking whether romantic love is merely an artistic sublimation of sexual attraction, or whether it is the expression of something much deeper in the human soul. She recognises that love can evoke powerful emotions and can cause chaos in the most prosaic life. In Mardy Grothe's book he quotes Peter de Vries: "Marriage is to courting as humming is to singing".

My visit to the book fair was rewarding. It extends my library incrementally, and nudges it in unforeseen directions.


# 7   About Personal Libraries

It has been a surprising experience, going to book fairs and looking for books that I already own. It brings me to asking the question, what reasons do people have for having a home library – or personal library, or private library? I wrote down all the reasons I could think of. There were quite a few.

The first reason was vanity. People build up their own library because it looks good to other people, say, visitors to their house. I remember that a friend of one of my sons visited our house, and afterwards, my son told me what his friend had said: "Your father has so many books!" And my son answered him, "This is not even the library. These are just the books that are in the house!"

We both laughed about that. I don't think my son thinks I keep books for reasons of vanity, meaning, focused on what other people think. But there are many varieties of vanity.

From several quarters I have heard the story about people who want a library because it looks impressive. It infers quietly that I have good taste and I know what is of value. Or that I have great knowledge. So, how does one acquire such a library? One measures the length of one's shelves, and then orders sufficient books of a suitable variety to fill that shelf length.

I heard that story from a tradesman who had built a house for some well-off people. I heard the same story at a book fair, from someone who was assigned to purchase a suitable array of books for a set of empty shelves. This is the economical approach, sensible because many of the books at book fairs look like new. And I had heard it from a bookstore point of view, where it was considered important to get a good-looking selection of books (new) across a suitable variety of subjects. And it is always a bonanza for the bookshop, because you can sneak in lots of books that have been difficult to sell.

I suppose my library fails in some socially important respects.

The strangest kind of library that I heard about was one that was sorted in terms of the colour of the spines. The people had taken time to do this, and they had searched for books to go in sections where the predominant colour of the spine would match the other books. Pink, orange, brown, black, black with gold printing, grey.

I try to imagine it. I have only come up with two categories; one is where the books are very old, say, hardbacks from the early twentieth century. The other is the Penguin classic editions of literary works, which all look remarkably the same: orange background, black print for the author and white print for the title. Only the title and author name differ between books. I have a few books from this phase, for example, Gabriel Garcia Marquez, *Love in the Time of Cholera* (1988).

However, even the Penguin Classics have gone through changes of style. I have two copies of J.D. Salinger's *The Catcher in the Rye*, one from 1951 and one from 1994, both from Penguin, and the style is quite different. I have a copy of Albert Camus' *The Outsider* from 2013, and although it is a Penguin Modern Classic, it would be difficult to shelve it stylistically with the other books just mentioned.

I suspect that, in the end, the enterprise is merely vain, although it could be called surprising, innovative or amusing. More to the point, it could be a vain enterprise in the sense that it would probably be futile to try to achieve it.

However, I have another perspective on this issue. I bought a painting (a print) from an artist I know. It was of a wall of books, one that you might see in a school or public library. A girl is sitting on the floor in front of it reading a book. What struck me about the painting was the richness of the colours on the spines of the books. It was a full palette of colours: browns, reds, greens, blues, orange, a little black, a little white, with a red carpet on the floor below. It is very satisfying to look at, so perhaps I do understand someone who set out to create an effect based on colours.

I bought the painting because I had created a wall for all my academic awards: degrees and so on. But I wanted to say that books are more important than the institutional awards. The painting did it for me. And then I was reading *I Never Metaphor I Didn't Like* and found just the right saying, so I could say it in words as well: "What we become depends on what we read after all of the professors have finished with us. The greatest university of all is a collection of books" (Thomas Carlyle). I printed that out and put it up on the wall as well.

Another common reason for having a library is out of dependence. This is a constellation of reasons, that include reliance on them, and comfort. A person feels the need to have the books around to refer to. The books constitute an authority, the authority, for whatever subjects are deemed important. If the person was religious, there would be religious books to refer to, or quote from, and that would be that!

Another reason? Nostalgia or sentimentality. For the person, the books represent a time in the past when the books were central. Perhaps the person was a student at school or university, and they were good years. The books remind them of the time. A different example: among her few books, my mother had a book about the coronation of Queen Elizabeth in 1953. The inside cover displays the family crest of the Royal Family, and there are many studio photos of the young queen, already looking responsible. Included are photos of Prince Charles, then three years old. It is a very comforting book.

A slightly different perspective is the idea of respect for antiquity or authority. Books can represent what is known, or what has been established and accepted. Against all the iconoclasts in society, given books can be a bulwark. Against all the threats that exist to stability, books stand ready to rebut and disclaim.

Or, a person may be by nature a student. They are inherently studious, whether or not they have a formal role anymore as a student. They like to explore and they like to learn, perhaps across many fields. It makes sense to surround themselves with books. If you are learning or testing your knowledge, you need books as a resource. This used to be the function of encyclopedias, although we seem to have grown out of that. Of course, the internet has had its part to play, but we are not yet over the need for books, for the physical, material objects.

Librarians may remind us that a book is also called a codex, meaning a compiled collection of pages bound together, as opposed to scrolls. The word 'codex' comes from the Latin 'caudex', meaning 'tree trunk', and derives from the fact that the first Roman law books were made from wooden tablets covered with wax and tied together with string.

In contrast to the student, other people may use books for entertainment or escape. Their libraries may be full of paperbacks on romance, westerns, detective stories or humour. The content of their libraries reflects their reasons for reading. "You can learn a lot about a person from what is in their library." Well, I apply that rule with a caution. There are books in my library because I thought I should know something about the subject. It does not imply that I agree with the author. For example, I bought a book on "intelligent design" because I had heard people talk about it and I wondered....

Are there other reasons for having a library? Indeed, there are. It could be a choice of interests, just as a person might decide to collect stamps, or kitchen scales, or ashtrays. I don't deny that any of these pursuits could turn out to be interesting. Collecting books is, among other things, a choice in how to spend one's time (and money). I must protest, however, that I have never thought of my growing library as me "collecting books".

"Collecting books" is an outsider's view, where the books are seen primarily as objects of some value. I think that most people who are committed to their library have an insider's perspective. For many years, when I was working as a commentator on management, I collected books on management and leadership. I was interested in what various writers had to say about the subject matter. I was following my interests, not seeking to build up an objectively impressive collection for the public eye. The public never knew, and still doesn't know, what books I have on the subject.

This leads to another reason for building a library, which is, to follow a particular subject. In this case, the person's library is not broad-based. They are not interested in having a well-balanced collection of books, only in acquiring more insights into their particular area of knowledge. Perhaps they are interested in traditional methods of Japanese woodwork, or the convict era in Van Diemen's Land. They are not interested in (or even aware of) books on other subjects.

I suppose, in a way, we are all like that. When I go to a book fair, I never look at the tables of books on cooking, military history or romance. I don't buy books on those subjects. But here, I am referring to people whose interests are much narrower than usual, and their libraries only contain books on the one subject. Years ago, there used to be publishers who only published books of historical literature, such as Charles Dickens and Jane Austen. I mean, a library consisting of that degree of specificity.

It must be said that some people have an affection for the books themselves. For this person, it is not just the subject matter that matters. They may be proud of the fact that they have five editions of Jane Austen's *Pride and Prejudice*, and every one of them is special. Perhaps one of them is even a first edition. Although I do take pleasure in these features, I do not go looking for them. My criterion is that the book must be relevant and functional – readable. I have many books that have been marked by the previous reader, with pencil or with a highlighter. I treasure this, because it gives me an insight into what someone else thought of the content.

Each of these reasons seems to connect to the following reason. So, an extension of the above reason is that the library-owner may want to have a connection to the author. Having a copy of *Pride and Prejudice* may be, for the person, a connection to Jane Austen. They may love her perspective and her turn of mind.

When I first started reading Christian books outside of my local sphere, I discovered C.H. Dodd, a Catholic writer in Britain, and I related to him because he gave me an entirely different perspective, outside of my childhood enclave, that I later built upon through other writers. I went on to discover Jacques Ellul, a French writer whose ideas are still salient to me fifty years later. A connection to an author may be a significant factor in the establishment of a library.

Yet another reason for having a library is that a book may be a memento of an occasion, or of events. Perhaps this is a rather specialised reason, but I can offer a few different examples. Again, back to my mother. On her shelves she had a book on the history of Rathdowney. Why? Did she come from there? No, she didn't. But she and her second husband, George, travelled in rural Australia a lot, and they purchased mementos of places where they went. Rathdowney is a tiny town near the New South Wales-Queensland border. (When I lived in Kyogle I could have travelled there in less than three hours.) So, the book purchase was a memento of their trip.

Another example is if you were given a book. I have a few books that I received at school as prizes. For example, *Great Short Stories of the World*, introduction by Gerda Charles, published 1964, was the book I received for being the Dux of the School in 1967. Perhaps it was the receipt of these books as prizes that was the germ of the idea of having a library. I can certainly claim that now.

Another kind of memento is if you went to the event that launched a book. I have been to numerous book launches. Some of the people were friends, so their books are, apart from anything else, mementos of the occasions. The first two books I wrote were on the history of Kyogle and of its school, and there were launch events for both. I am sure that for many people who bought the books, the book represented a memento of the occasion rather than a reference for their study of local history.

I have not numbered all my reasons, but I could note that this next reason is the twelfth: the library is a form of stewardship of knowledge or culture. Just like my library of management books. If I needed to write an article about management, I could peruse my volumes and choose what I wanted to say. If I wanted to guide someone on what was worth reading, I could do that too.

The extension of the above reason is having a library specifically as a resource for training and education. If you have to teach on a topic or put together a training course, books are a resource for that purpose. And I do find pleasure in writing a course and being surrounded by open books, choosing which ones to refer to and what concepts to use. We all draw from others. Once, I heard a person say, whimsically, that the only original people were Adam and Eve. Everything since then has been derivative and collaborative.

I offer the comment whimsically, because I think occasionally people do come up with original ideas. But even when an idea is original, the elaboration of that idea inevitably involves recourse to existing materials. Hence, one needs a library.

So, lastly, reason number fourteen: a library is a way of sharing ideas. What do I mean? Well, the assumption is that one allows other people to enter one's library and browse. Then, in conversation, one may find there are books in the library that are a conduit to follow.

Generally, I find that this is the case. Just as going to book fairs continues to extend the scope of my library, talking to other people in the environment of the library enables ideas to spill out and interweave.

# 8   Learning and the Library

Has my perspective changed or grown as a result of my discoveries at recent book fairs? One perspective that has been refreshed is my journey across time. I discovered *Green Mountains* and it reminded me vividly of my first major book project, writing the history of the Kyogle Shire in 1988. Sometimes it's good to ask, what do I think about that now? And I feel thankful for what was accomplished then, and the offering it was to a place I loved. "Gratitude is the heart's memory."

There were numerous books I found that took me back into the period of time when I was working on the book *Future: A Spiritual Story of Humanity*. I think this is because there is more to be said on this subject and I will probably come back to it. Were there things I didn't say, or didn't say clearly enough? Is there more that I want to say? Or have I changed my mind about what I said?

It's enough that I raise those questions now. I'm not sure that I could answer them yet. But there is another question: do I have enough books in my library to work on this topic? The answer to that is always yes, but it's like having a garden full of flowers, but then you go out and find something that is just lovely and it would be great to have that too. It would embellish the final picture.

There were books I found that are pertinent to my immersion in my family's history. Once I thought general history was remote from me and my family; now I think I am connected to all of it – like it or not.

The book on London in the eighteenth and early nineteenth centuries is relevant to all of my ancestors, even the ones who came from elsewhere than London: Cornwall, Scotland, Ireland, Hertfordshire, Oxfordshire. London told the dominant story; the other places were subject to it or influenced by it.

Several of the books I found could be described as New Age, although I dislike the term. When I lived on the far north coast and my hair and beard were long, I was called a hippie. But I would look at other 'hippies' and think, I am nothing like you. It was a case of external appearance trumping any effort to countenance complexity. Just so, there are "New Age" books I can relate to, and others that I think are cheap, gratuitous or irrelevant.

Seeing these books enabled me to revisit my views. Some books continue to be "fellow travellers", good companions, others not so much. It's like the fracas about the word 'spirituality'. In some contexts it helps to identify a core value in life; at other times it just confuses things.

A while ago, I was asked what my beliefs were, by a man who had a very structured set of beliefs. The questions of meaning and of right and wrong were answered for him by a catechism subscribed to by a host of other people. He can recite the expression of this meaning with confidence, precision and passion. In this he is in solidarity with a group of other people.

I have no affiliation with an organisation that has an organised point of view. Each time I answer this question I find new angles instead. My answer is made up of a million moments of insights, thousands of books and conversations, and dozens of periods of engagement with specific philosophers, religions, and programs of self-improvement. Some elements of my world view have been constant and are never in doubt. Some elements of my understanding evolve, and sometimes the tide of experience gathers up elements I have not addressed and turns them over, pushes them away, or buries them in the sand while revealing clearer truths.

The beginning of my understanding is the realisation that I am here as a living creature in a world, with a desire to live and a capacity to think about life and its meaning. That realisation goes back to early childhood. This is the beginning of the ceaseless striving to make sense of who I am, that lives hand-in-hand with the already-present sense of wonder about all-that-is, and the desire to enjoy life and feel good. And in parallel, the desire not to harm the earth.

Other people clearly strive from different places.

Even the question, I now realise, is wrong. Belief in the primacy of belief lends itself to argument, and to the position: I am right and you are wrong. But I am aware that I have discussed the nature of belief previously, in several places. Am I confused? Have I tried to have it several different ways?

This is a possibility. I thought of a saying many years ago: "The definition of immaturity is that one has beliefs that contradict each other, and one is unaware of that." And, the more immature one is, the more such beliefs exist. Immaturity is not yet seeing that we are part of the whole, that everything has to be integrated.

You could say it is an expression of the statement that an unexamined life is not worth living. If Mardy Grothe had heard my saying, he might have put it in his book.

So, let us resolve this issue of beliefs. On the one hand, beliefs are real and important. Deepak Chopra says, "Belief creates biology." For example, there are social, collective beliefs about aging, and we fall into them by default. It takes work to identify these beliefs and separate ourselves from them. Similarly, Bruce Lipton says our beliefs can be self-limiting. We need to shift to a sense of empowerment over our own life.

Don Miguel Ruiz (*The Four Agreements*) addresses the same issue. If you have always thought you were lacking, can you just tell yourself the opposite? It is not so simple; the first belief has been living in your mind for quite a while, so it takes work to replace it with another belief. We are dealing with the habits of our reasoning mind.

It is Buddhism that makes the strongest argument that belief is not the most important function. Buddha asserts that we improve our lives by the way we live, through living in peace and tranquillity, practising silence, stillness and meditation, discipline, love, and non-judgement. Rick Rubin's book on how to cultivate creativity advocates similar practices. It is where we put our energy that makes a difference.

Deepak Chopra says, your beliefs pertain to how you feel about reality: how you feel. I think that says it all. Beliefs are not outside of your control, and your feelings are not outside of your control, and your feelings are not the plaything of your reason. It could be that it is more the other way round. And I think that is enough to say about that. You have to work on it. Having the "correct belief" (a creed) is not the answer: "The name that can be named is not the eternal name" (*Tao Te Ching*).

The most recurrent theme in the books I discovered is "how to live". Are all these books necessary? Are they all helpful? I hope that my exploration of these books has shown what help they may be. Has too much been said? Probably, but then again, possibly not.

I read a book on Zen Buddhism by Osho. There is a story in it about Buddha, surrounded by thousands of people who had come to hear him talk. But he did not talk. He sat there holding a flower. Time went by, and many people became restless. One man, Mahakashyap, could restrain himself no longer, and he laughed. Buddha beckoned him to come near, and he gave him the flower. He said to the crowd, "All that can be given in words I have given to you, but with this flower I give to Mahakashyap the key to all the teachings."

The key cannot be delivered through words, or through the mind. And yet, Osho has written a whole book to explain Zen Buddhism. This is the conundrum. We are complex beings. We have bodies, minds, emotions, social networks, societies. This is apart from particular fields of knowledge: chemistry, physics, mathematics, geology, history, and technical expertise. And at the heart of it is consciousness, like a patient dragon.

Barbara Tuchman, an American historian and writer, said, "Books are the carriers of civilisation. Without books, history is silent, literature dumb, science crippled, thought and speculation at a standstill."

But then we have a new conundrum, the rediscovery of indigenous thinking. The journey is not ended. Books may be vehicles, but they are not the destination. The object is not the books themselves.

# Bibliography

---, *Antique Maps: Library of Congress*, 1999, Pomegranate, Rohnert Park CA.

---, *Sydney and the Bush*, 1980, New South Wales Education Department, Sydney.

---, *Great Short Stories of the World*, 1964, introduction by Gerda Charles, Spring Books, London.

---, *The Shorter Oxford English Dictionary*, 1962 (1933), prepared by William Little, revised and edited by C.T. Onions, third edition, Oxford University Press, London.

Armstrong, Karen, *Fields of Blood*, 2014, The Bodley Head, London.

Austen, Jane, *Pride and Prejudice*, 1992 (1813), Wordsworth Classics, Ware, Hertfordshire.

Austen, Jane, *Pride and Prejudice*, 2015 (1813), Barnes & Noble, New York.

Bakewell, Sarah, *The English Dane*, 2005, Vintage, Sydney.

Battles, Matthew, *Library: An Unquiet History*, 2003, Vintage, Sydney.

Behrens, Peter, *The Law of Dreams*, 2006, Text Publishing Company, Melbourne.

Benson, Herbert, *Timeless Healing*, 1996, Hodder & Stoughton, Sydney.

Bryson, Bill, *A Short History of Nearly Everything*, 2003, Transworld, London.

Byrne, Rhonda, *The Secret*, 2006, Atria Books, New York.

Camus, Albert, *The Outsider*, 2013 (1942), translated by Sandra Smith, Penguin Modern Classic, London.

Chodron, Pema, *When Things Fall Apart*, 1997, Shambhala, Boston.

Chopra, Deepak, *Ageless Body, Timeless Mind*, 1993, Rider, London.

Chopra, Deepak, *Living in the Light*, 2023, Rider, London.

Chopra, Deepak, *Quantum Healing*, 2015 (1989), Bantam Books, New York.

Civaschi, Matteo, *Life in Five Seconds: Over 200 Stories for Those with No Time to Waste*, 2012, Quercus, London.

Courtenay, Bryce, *The Power of One*, 1996, Ballantyne Books.

Covey, Stephen, *Seven Habits of Highly Effective People*, 1989, Free Press, New York.

Covey, Stephen, *The Eighth Habit*, 2004, Free Press, New York.

Dalai Lama, *Ancient Wisdom, Modern World: Ethics for the New Millennium*, 1999, Abacus, London.

Dalai Lama, *The Art of Happiness: A Handbook for Living*, 1998, Hodder & Stoughton, Sydney.

de Boinod, Adam Jacot, *The Meaning of Tingo*, 2005, Penguin, London.

de Botton, Alain, *The Consolations of Philosophy*, 2000, Penguin, Melbourne.

de Botton, Alain, *The Pleasures and Sorrows of Work*, 2009, Hamish Hamilton, Camberwell VIC.

Dispenza, Joe, *Becoming Supernatural*, 2017, Hay House Australia, Sydney.

Drabble, Margaret, *Oxford Companion to English Literature*, 1991, Oxford University Press, London.

Fenton-Smith, Paul, *Intuition*, 2011, Academy Publishing, Yatala QLD.

Fenton-Smith, Paul, *A Secret Door to the Universe*, 1999, Simon & Schuster, Sydney.

Fidler, Richard and Kari Gislason, *Sagaland*, 2017, Harper Collins, Sydney.

Flanagan, Kitty, *488 Rules for Life*, 2019, Allen & Unwin, Sydney.

Fluck, Edward J., translator, *A Dictionary of Platitudes*, 1954, (from Gustave Flaubert, *A Dictionary of Received Ideas,* 1913), Rodale Press, Emmaus PA.

Frankl, Viktor, *Man's Search for Meaning*, 1989 (1946), Pocket Books, New York.

Gammage, Bill, *The Biggest Estate on Earth,* 2011, Allen & Unwin, Sydney.

Gawande, Atul, *Being Mortal*, 2014, Profile Books, London.

Gawande, Atul, *The Checklist Manifesto: How to Get Things Right,* 2016, Picador, New York.

Georg, Eugen, *The Adventure of Mankind,* 1931, translated from the German by Robert Bek-Gran, E.P. Dutton & Co., New York.

Gibran, Kahlil, *Nymphs of the Valley*, 1948, William Heinemann, Melbourne.

Gibran, Kahlil, *The Prophet,* 1971 (1926), Willliam Heinemann, London.

Gilbert, Elizabeth, *Committed: A Love Story*, 2010, Bloomsbury, London.

Gilbert, Elizabeth, *The Signature of all Things*, 2013, Bloomsbury, London.

Goldberg, Natalie, *Writing down the Bones: Freeing the Writer Within*, 2005, Shambhala, Boston.

Gombrich, E.H., *A Little History of the World*, 2008 (1936), translated by Caroline Mustill, Yale University Press, New Haven CT.

Gombrich, E.H., *A Little History of the World*, 2008 (1936), illustrated edition, translated by Caroline Mustill, Yale University Press, New Haven CT.

Grace, Annie, *The Alcohol Experiment*, 2020, Avery, New York.

Grainger, Elena, *Martin of Martin Place*, 1970, Alpha Books, Sydney.

Grant, Stan, *Talking to My Country*, 2016, Harper Collins, Sydney.

Greene, Graham, *The Quiet American*, 1973, Penguin Twentieth Century Classic, London.

Grothe, Mardy, *I Never Metaphor I Didn't Like*, 2008, Harper Collins, New York.

Hancock, Graham, *Fingerprints of the Gods*, 1995, Three Rivers Press, London.

Hancock, Graham, *Magicians of the Gods*, 2016, Coronet, London.

Hay, Louise, *You Can Heal Your Life*, 1987, Specialist Publications, Sydney.

Hitchcock, Tim and Robert Shoemaker, *London Lives: Poverty, Crime and the Making of a Modern City, 1690-1800*, 2015, Cambridge University Press, Cambridge.

Honore, Carl, *In Praise of Slowness: Challenging the Cult of Speed*, 2005, Harper One, New York.

Hopkins, Andrea, *The Book of Courtly Love*, 1994, Aquarian Books, London.

Hua-Ching Ni, *Eight Thousand Years of Chinese Wisdom*, 1983, Seven Star Communications, Santa Monica CA.

Jullien, Francois, *A Treatise on Efficacy: Between Western and Chinese Thinking*, 2004, translated by Janet Lloyd, University of Hawaii Press, Honolulu.

Kasparov, Garry, *Deep Thinking: Where Machine Intelligence Ends*, 2017, John Murray, London.

Lao Tsu, *Tao Te Ching,* 2006, translated by Stephen Mitchell, Harper Perennial Modern Classics, New York.

Le Guin, Ursula, *The Word for World is Forest*, 1972, Orion Books, London.

Leece, Germaine and Sonya Tsakalakis, *Reading the Seasons*, 2021, Thames & Hudson Australia, Melbourne.

Lencioni, Patrick, *The Five Dysfunctions of a Team*, 2002, Jossey-Bass, San Francisco.

Lencioni, Patrick, *The Five Temptations of a CEO*, 2008, John Wiley, New York.

Lencioni, Patrick, *The Four Obsessions of an Extraordinary Executive*. 2000, John Wiley, New York.

Leunig, Michael, *The Curly Pyjama Letters*, 2001, Penguin, Melbourne.

Lin Yutang, *The Importance of Living*, 1952, Willliam Heinemann, Melbourne.

Lipton, Bruce, *The Biology of Belief*, 2011, Hay House Australia, Sydney.

Low, Tim, *Where Song Began*, 2017, Penguin, Sydney.

Marquez, Gabriel Garcia, *Love in the Time of Cholera,* 1988 (1985), Penguin, London.

Marryat, Captain Frederick, *Children of the New Forest,* 1994 (1847), Bloomsbury, London.

O'Reilly, Bernard, *Green Mountains*, 1940, printed by W.R. Smith & Paterson, Brisbane.

O'Reilly, Bernard, *Green Mountains*, c1975, Envirobook, Sydney.

Oriah Mountain Dreamer, *The Invitation*, 1999, Harper One, New York.

Oriah Mountain Dreamer, *What We Ache For,* 2005, Harper, San Francisco.

Osho, *Zen: Its History and Teachings*, 2004, Ixos Press, Lewes, UK.

Pascoe, Bruce, *Dark Emu*, 2014, Magabala Books, WA.

Peck, M. Scott, *The Different Drum*, 1983, Rider, London.

Peck, M. Scott, *The Road Less Travelled*, 2020 (1978), Rider, London.

Peterson, Jordan, *Twelve Rules for Life*, 2018, Allen Lane, Melbourne.

Piper, Ailsa, *Sinning across Spain*, 2012, Victory Books, Melbourne.

Piper, Ailsa and Tony Doherty, *The Attachment: Letters from a Most Unlikely Friendship*, 2017, Allen & Unwin, Sydney.

Prentis, Malcolm, *The Scots in Australia*, 2008, UNSW Press, Sydney.

Prochnik, Geoge, *The Impossible Exile: Stefan Zweig at the End of the World*, 2014, Other Press, New York.

Richmond, Lewis, *Every Breath, New Chances: How to Age with Honour and Dignity, A Guide for Men*, 2020, North Atlantic Books, Berkley CA.

Robinson, Ken, *The Element: How finding Your Passion Changes Everything*, 2009, Allen Lane, Camberwell VIC.

Robson, Lloyd, *A Short History of Tasmania*, 1997, Oxford University Press, Melbourne.

Rookmaaker, H.R., *Modern Art and the Death of a Culture*, 1970, Inter-Varsity Press, London.

Roszak, Theodore, *The Making of the Counter Culture*, 1972, Faber & Faber, London.

Royce, Josiah, *The Philosophy of Loyalty*, 2018 (1908), Forgotten Books, London.

Rubin, Rick, *The Creative Act: A Way of Being*, 2023, Canongate, Edinburgh.

Rudd, Richard, 2015, *Gene Keys*, Watkins, London.

Ruiz, Don Miguel, *The Four Agreements: Companion Volume*, 1997, Amber-Allen, San Rafael CA.

Salinger, J.D., *The Catcher in the Rye*, 1951, Penguin, London.

Salinger, J.D., *The Catcher in the Rye*, 1994, Penguin, London.

Satir, Virginia, *Peoplemaking*, 1972, Science and Behavior Books, Palo Alto CA.

Smart, Simon, editor, *A Spectator's Guide to Worldviews*, 2016, third edition, Aquila Press, Sydney.

Stable, J.J., editor, *The Bond of Poetry: A Book of Verse for Australian Schools*, 1939, Oxford University Press, Melbourne.

Tan Twan Eng, *The Garden of Evening Mists*, 2012, Myrmidon, Newcastle-upon-Tyne.

Truss, Lynne, *Eats, Shoots and Leaves*, 2003, Profile Books, London.

Van Loon, Hendrik Willem, *The Story of Mankind*, 1941 (1922), George Harrap, London.

Van Loon, Hendrik Willem, *The Story of Mankind*, 1999 (1922), Liveright, New York.

Vernon, Mark, *After Atheism*, 2007, Palgrave Macmillan, Basingstoke, Hampshire.

Welsh, Frank, *Great Southern Land*, 2005, Penguin, Melbourne.

White, Suzanne, *The New Chinese Astrology*, 1993, Pan Books, London.

Wilde, Oscar, *Lord Arthur Savile's Crime: A Study of Duty*, c1946 (1891), Joseph Waters, Melbourne.

Young, Damon, *Philosophy in the Garden*, 2012, Melbourne University Press, Melbourne.

Young-Eisendrath, Polly, *The Self-Esteem Trap*, 2008, Little Brown & Co, New York.

Yunkaporta, Tyson, *Sand Talk: How Indigenous Thinking Can Save the World*, 2019, Text Publishing Company, Melbourne.

Zuckerman, Andrew, *Wisdom: Peace*, 2009, Harry N. Abrams, New York.

## About the Author

**Glenn Martin** lives in Sydney, although he lived in the bush on the far north coast of New South Wales for two decades. He has been a teacher at high schools and tertiary institutions, a manager of community services organisations, and a commentator on management, business ethics, employment law, and training and development. He has been the editor of publications for management and training professionals and an instructional designer for online learning. He is the author of over twenty books.

www.ingramcontent.com/pod-product-compliance
Lightning Source LLC
Chambersburg PA
CBHW060512090426
42735CB00011B/2188